Instant TIME MANAGEMENT

BRIAN CLEGG

KOGAN PAGE

To Gillian, Chelsea and Rebecca
for making my time worth organizing.

YOURS TO HAVE AND TO HOLD

BUT NOT TO COPY

First published in 1999
Reprinted in 1999

Kogan Page Limited
120 Pentonville Road
London
N1 9JN
UK

Stylus Publishing Inc.
22883 Quicksilver Drive
Sterling
VA 20166-2012
USA

© Brian Clegg, 1999

British Library Cataloguing in Publication Data

A CIP record for this book is available from the British Library.

ISBN 0 7494 2963 1

Contents

4 The exercises 23

5 Other sources 97

Appendix 1: the framework 103

Appendix 2: the selector   109

1

TIME MANAGEMENT

SYSTEMATIC FAILURE

Time management is a discipline that everyone acknowledges is worthwhile while simultaneously ignoring it. There seems to be something in the human spirit that rebels against time management, despite realizing the benefits. It's rather like eating the right food – we can acknowledge all the benefits of eating lots of fruit and vegetables, we can even enjoy eating fruit and vegetables – and still pig out on junk food.

This ability to ignore time management is very sad. There are plenty of variations on the theme of 'so much to do, so little time to do it in'. Few of us have time to get everything we really want to do completed. Few of us manage to effectively balance work and home life, business and pleasure, stress and stress relief. Good time management is more than a nit-picking discipline that will appeal to those who like everything in its place; it is a vehicle for getting more done and having a better life. If only it can be made practical.

This book makes time management practical by using the *Instant* approach of providing a package of quick to read, quick to implement ideas that can be started right away. In effect, it applies time management to time management. One of the big time management messages is not to try to do everything at once, but to take on tasks in bite-sized chunks; this book provides just that, time management, a bite at a time.

IT DOESN'T EXIST

Having established the value of time management, if only we could find the time to do it, it's rather unfortunate that there is no such thing. It can't be done – it simply doesn't exist. Remember Lewis Carroll's masterly summary of the problems of dealing with time:

Alice sighed wearily. 'I think you might do something better with the time,' she said, 'than wasting it in asking riddles that have no answers.'

'If you knew time as well as I do,' said the Hatter, 'you wouldn't talk about wasting it. It's him.'

'I don't know what you mean,' said Alice.

'Of course you don't!' the Hatter said, tossing his head contemptuously. 'I dare say you never even spoke to Time!'

'Perhaps not,' Alice cautiously replied; 'but I know I have to beat time when I learn music.'

'Ah! That accounts for it,' said the Hatter. 'He won't stand beating. Now, if you only kept on good terms with him, he'd do almost anything you liked with the clock. For instance, suppose it were nine o'clock in the morning, just time to begin lessons: you'd only have to whisper a hint to Time, and round goes the clock in a twinkling! Half-past one, time for dinner!'

Alice in Wonderland

Time is not amenable to management, nor to argument; it continues to tick away at an irritatingly constant sixty seconds a minute, for sixty minutes per hour.

If that were all there were to it, this would be an extremely short book, but there's more. Objective time may be utterly beyond control, but subjective time is much more variable. Your attitude to what you are doing has a huge effect on the passage of subjective time, being capable of slowing it to a crawl or speeding it up immensely. More usefully, we can generally influence the demands on our time – both in quantity and execution – and the effectiveness with which we use the time we've got. Time management might be impossible, but resource management certainly isn't. You'll find throughout this book that the term 'time management' is used for convenience – but bear in mind that it's a useful fiction.

YOU CAN'T WASTE IT...

There hardly seems to be a day goes by without another report from a group of pompous management consultants announcing how much time office workers waste on something or other. Flavour of the month is surfing the Internet, but once that goes away, something else will emerge. This is a shame, because with the possible exception of spending it on writing reports like those, you can't waste time any more than you can manage it.

What you can do, is to give relative weightings to the different activities you could have undertaken in that particular chunk of time. This is not a trivial activity, which is why such reports are so misleading. The weighting you give to an activity is dependent on many things. For instance, it is time dependent. Say you were approaching the deadline for completing a major piece of work. The courier is standing waiting for you to finish. The board is about to meet to discuss your recommendations. It is not a good move to put everything to one side and start looking for your passport, which you are going to need for your holiday three months later. However, come the morning of the holiday, looking for that passport will be rather higher up your priorities. It's obvious, isn't it? Yet very few of us make such prioritization competently.

The attitude you have to an activity also depends strongly on its outcomes and linkages, some of which are not always easily seen. A classic advertisement for *The Guardian* newspaper showed an obvious thug pushing over a poor, defenceless person. It was the sort of thing that made you want to bring back corporal punishment. Then it showed the same scene from a different angle. Now you saw the danger that was facing the poor defenceless person, and how the apparent thug's push had saved them from harm. So-called time wasting is sometimes like this. Yes, that Internet browsing could be purely recreational, but equally it could glean some information that is valuable to the business.

A final consideration in the weightings is the balance between business and social demands. A more accurate interpretation of what is often labelled time wasting is 'time spent on social activity which could be spent on business'. Note that this is not a justification for undertaking social activities in office hours, just a more useful description of what is happening.

... BUT YOU CAN MANAGE DEMANDS AND USAGE

If time can't be managed or wasted, what's the point? Time management is about taking control of the demands that are made on your available time. About ensuring that the use you make of your time – a very limited allocation – has the best fit with your personal goals and requirements. It is about saying 'no' where it's appropriate to other people, to non-human time eaters and to yourself. It is about getting the right balance. For this reason, the first requirement in setting about time management is not to get your diary sorted or your desk tidy, it is to establish just what your personal goals are – without being clear about these you have no frame of reference in which to allocate time.

When achieving a balance, remember the importance of both business and social demands. Often we assume that business must always have the priority. A director of a UK corporate once commented that it was a shame he hadn't had the chance to see his children growing up, but the pressures of work didn't allow him much contact with them. If he had taken a wider view of time management, he would have realized that he could legitimately allocate more time to his family. So many people miss out on a social life, yet will say that they are working 'for the family' – the balance simply isn't right. This is not to say that the social life must always come first, or that it is somehow wrong to have your career as a central driving force of your life – just that time management has to take in a bigger picture.

As you use the exercises and techniques you will find many different ways to improve time management, but there is one approach that is so fundamental that it is worth bringing up straight away. Time management is often about dealing with big tasks – activities that can take over, given the chance. The magic wand that the good time manager can wave to overcome these rampant tasks is chunking. Breaking up a task into manageable chunks is an absolute essential for time management. After all, the whole business of balancing your time is rather like juggling. These big tasks are equivalent to trying to juggle with cars – it's impossible. However, by breaking them up, you are reduced to juggling with wing mirrors or steering wheels, a much more practical possibility. Dealing with a single large task without breaking it down is difficult enough – dealing with many large tasks, both business and social, is an impossibility.

This need to break up major tasks into chunks may seem obvious, but when you are faced with a big job it is all too easy to plunge in. Time is short; you need to get started. Taking the (brief) time required to break down the task into chunks will pay back handsomely, but it is a very human failing not to do so.

THE INFLUENCES

A popular phrase (it would be generous to call it a joke) in any service business is 'it would be a great job if it wasn't for the customers'. Time management is a bit like this. It would be extremely easy, if it wasn't for all the factors that conspire to stop you from being organized.

The first, and perhaps biggest factor is you yourself. As we have already noted, most people have an in-built aversion to time management. You might have a very clear picture of what you want to achieve today, and how you are going to do it. Unfortunately, soon after starting you get a craving for a chocolate bar which sends you down to the shop. Then you get distracted, thinking about something you should have done last weekend, or the holiday you are planning. Then you decide you had better check the post. Somehow most of the day has slipped away without you ever getting started.

If this weren't bad enough, there are the other people, too. Just popping in for a chat, or asking for some information right away, even though it is going to take you three hours to collect it, and you are already working on another urgent project. There are the phone calls and e-mails, the cries for help and the demands for attention. People are out to capture your time whenever they can. Other people aren't always negative contributors, of course. Delegation is a highly effective time management tool, as long as you resist the urge to constantly monitor the activity. People can free up time for you, if you can go about it the right way.

Even without other people, the rest of the world is capable of eating away at your available time. Just the smell of fresh coffee or hot rolls can be enough to distract. Technology can be a great time consumer. PCs are wonderful business tools, but they are also a temptation to tinker. I'll get that important memo written when I've just got my desktop arranged the way I want it. Oh, and while I'm at it, I'll just delete a few files I don't need any more. And install that new program off the magazine cover disk. Don't forget technology's ability to be a positive aid, though. Sending off a quick e-mail when an idea occurs to you will both free up your mental resources and be a lot quicker than writing, printing and sending a letter. Technology is a first class two-edged sword.

All of the exercises and techniques in this book are about modifying or controlling these influences. Bringing them into line to help to make your use of your time more effective and satisfying.

WHY INSTANT?

There is probably no area more appropriate for the instant approach than time management. Some time management systems, started with the best of intentions, have grown so complex that simply using the system is itself a major consumer of your time. The techniques and exercises in this book are designed to be used quickly – in a few spare minutes – so that the cure isn't worse than the problem.

Similarly, another problem with some approaches to time management is the need for revolution. You attend the seminar and get all fired up by the amazing time savings you will achieve, then come back to the office and get the usual wave of extra work and chaos dumped in your lap. You don't have time to implement your grand time management plan right now, so you put it on the shelf, ready to start tomorrow. Only things continue to be busy, so make that next week. Before you know it, your time management plan is growing a layer of dust that's thicker than the original document. The 'instant' aspect of this book is essential, because it makes it possible to introduce time management insidiously. By slipping in a very short exercise here and there, you can sneak up on yourself and get your time managed without realizing it.

FACING REALITY

There is one real problem, even if you manage to do everything this book suggests. That's the difference between perception and reality. You might know very well that you work best from mid-afternoon to mid-evening at a desk covered in pizza boxes, wearing torn jeans and listening to rock music. However, if your boss has the perception that to be a good worker you have to conform to standards of dress and time-keeping, it doesn't honestly matter how good your time management is, you are still going to suffer. This isn't fair, but it is very real.

Like it or not, having the appearance of being effective is just as important as actually getting the job done. Ideally, you ought to be able to do things your own way, but bear in mind that redundancies often come the way of those who are considered non-conformist, however good they are at their job. The changing face of work is mitigating this problem to some extent. As more and more people spend time working at home, for instance, they have a much better opportunity to work the way they want to, rather than the way their boss wants them to. Even so, it is essential to be politically and socially aware to survive. You will find, therefore, that some of the recommendations for time management – like overcoming the myth of the tidy desk – do need modifying to suit your particular environment.

USING THIS BOOK

Each exercise is presented in a standard format, with brief details of any preparation required, running time, resources used and the timescale of its application, followed by a description of the exercise itself. Next come suggestions for feedback, comments on the outcome and possible variations on the technique. The final part of the entry is the star rating. This is a quick reference to show which of the main influences on your time this particular exercise will impact, how much it applies to business and social time, and how much fun it is likely to be. As much as possible, to keep with the 'instant' theme, the exercises require minimal preparation, but some exercises requiring a little more work beforehand are included as they can sometimes be particularly effective. Note that timings are a minimum – you can take longer over most of the exercises if it is appropriate.

How you use the exercises very much depends on your approach to life (and time management). Some are better than others for a particular requirement. The tables in Appendix 2 offer a number of ways of picking an exercise. There is a random selection table as a way of dipping into the exercises without getting into a rut. There are tables arranging the exercises by how well they scored in the various star ratings. Appendix 1 contains suggestions for daily, weekly, monthly and annual programmes of the exercises which need regular repetition. And there is a day-by-day checklist. The exercises are arranged so that it is possible to work through them using one a day and so providing a regime that builds through the book. If you choose to use the book this way, the checklist will help you keep track of progress.

Such a formal approach might be useful if you have trouble finding time for time management – but bear in mind that one of the great benefits of a book like this is being able to dip in when you have a few minutes to spare. Don't let any structure you decide to impose get in the way of spontaneity.

2

MANAGING YOURSELF

WHY DO WE FIGHT IT?

Time management is mostly common sense. So why is it such a problem? It's almost as if there's something inside us that rebels against it. In fact, there's a whole bunch of reasons that conspire to make our time management fail. One is a leftover from our teens. Most teenagers spend a fair amount of time being told what they should do when, and they don't like it. Because time management can be seen as an imposed control on our time, it kicks in the urge to fight back, to refuse stubbornly what is obviously good for you just for the sake of it.

Another problem is laziness. Like it or not, most of us are lazy. We can't be bothered with the whole thing. We aren't very enthusiastic about change. And anyway, it's just an admin matter, isn't it? It's not exciting, important stuff, like creating or selling or whatever we like doing best – it's routine. Yawn.

Then there is the swamps and alligators problem. The old saying goes something like 'when you are up to your armpits (substitute part of the anatomy of your choice) in alligators, it's hard to think about draining the swamp'. Of course I'll get my time management sorted out, but wait until this crisis is out of the way. When I've got some time, I'll do something about it. Only thanks to a lack of time management, we never get the time, because there's always some new crisis, some new pressure.

Finally, there's the misconception that is fostered by some well-meaning approaches to time management. The fallacy that time management is closely related to having a neat, tidy desk and a well ordered filing system. The fact is, the way we work most effectively is a very personal thing. You can't take a 'one size fits all' approach to working. For some, having a clear desk and everything labelled and in its place is an essential – but it would be a mistake to say that this is the solution for everyone.

BEING COMFORTABLE

An essential start down the road of managing your own contribution to time management is being comfortable. This isn't a matter of getting a comfy chair with arm rests at the right height and all the rest (though it's not a bad idea), it's about being comfortable with the time management environment. If having a clear desk helps you to feel comfortable in your work, that's fine. If piles of clutter make you comfortable, that's fine too. Probably.

Probably, because there are two types of clutter. Mess becomes a problem for time management when it gets in the way. When you can't work properly because of the clutter. Most importantly when you can't find something because it's somewhere in one of ten huge piles. If, however, like many clutter lovers you can genuinely say 'it might be a mess, but I know where everything is', stick with it. Your clutter is your filing system. Clearing it up will just result in things going missing.

If you are a naturally tidy person, that's great, but don't feel too smug. The chances are that those who can say 'it might be a mess, but I know where everything is' have a more natural system – the brain, after all, doesn't store things in neat compartments. A loose, flowing system can cope better with a complex mix of information than a rigid matrix. You might be able to put your hands on any document in under a minute, but your colleague with a cluttered desk could probably produce the 10 most important documents of the moment in a couple of seconds.

This isn't a plea for clutter. Just a request that you adopt the approach to working with which you are most comfortable. If you like a mess, make sure it's a structured mess. If you like tidiness, make sure it doesn't result in the most frequently used items being as hard to get to as something you only need once a year.

ON THE EDGE OF THE ABYSS

You can't manage your time effectively unless you understand why you want to have time in the first place. A number of the early exercises in the book are about understanding the drivers that make you do things. What do you like doing? What would you like to be doing more (and less) of? What is it all for? If these sort of questions seem a trifle philosophical for a practical book like this, remember that time management isn't just there to make you better organized. You can't waste time, just use it with a more effective fit to your requirements. It's rather handy, therefore, to be aware of just what your requirements are before getting started.

The inevitable implication of this is that time management extends into your private life just as much as your working life. For some, this seems an intrusion. After all, this is a 'work' subject. It should stay in its little compartment, and leave my private life alone. This would be fine if you had such clear compartments. The fact is, your private life strays into work, your work life strays into the home, and you may well have many out-of-work interests which all clash with each other. Time hasn't any natural divisions – you have to impose them.

As we've already seen with the example of the busy director, more often than not it's business that encroaches on your private time. Not necessarily because someone else has forced it to. More often than not, because you have allowed it. Because you haven't thought through your priorities, and just what you are doing, you have allowed a combination of company culture and the inherent urgency of business to impose a totally unnatural set of priorities on you. Facing up to your own contribution to time mismanagement is an essential feature.

NOT LETTING GO

A particular danger for some personality types is over-monitoring. Many of us can't just let something go and expect a result. You have to keep checking and tinkering all the time. This can be particularly dangerous for those with subordinates. If you delegate a task, it's fine to set milestones and expect updates. But it's a disaster if you are constantly on top of those doing the work, getting in the way of anything being done. It is the classic problem for the small-time entrepreneur whose business is growing. He or she has to take on staff, but won't trust them to get on with the job. It is seen equally often when a junior manager starts to have staff.

If you are to make sensible use of your time, you have to be prepared to let go. Not entirely – you still have an interest. But you need to find ways to get the essential information as quickly as possible, at appropriate intervals, without interfering with the running of the business, and without distracting you from what you really should be doing.

Sometimes, managers don't delegate a task because it's not important enough. This seems crazy when stated so bluntly, but that's what happens. Your staff are all experts, with plenty to do. Here's a simple enough task, so you might as well do it and let them get on with their real work. There's an element of reality in this. If you are a manager of highly professional staff, it ought to be part of your role to deflect the garbage from them. Ideally, though, you should be deflecting it to someone else (or even better making sure it never gets done at all).

The one exception is where that task happens to overlap with a personal interest of yours and, as such, you can legitimately take it on because it is fulfilling other needs. When I ran the personal computer centre of a large corporate, my 30+ staff were kept frenetically busy supporting 10,000 or so users. When an opportunity came to sell off old PCs to staff, I handled it myself. I did this, because I really wanted to get PCs out to the people who worked for the company, just as I gave up some leisure time to give talks to the Computer Club. It was a task that I got something out of personally: if it hadn't been, I should have dropped it like a red hot brick.

BIOLOGICAL NEEDS

It's not something we're always comfortable about discussing, but there are biological needs which will impact on your time, too. Eating, sleeping, overcoming illness and more are going to have effects on your schedule. Ignore them at your peril. This isn't the right book to look at good diet or your sleeping patterns, but if you really want to get the most out of life it doesn't make sense to ignore your bodily needs.

One aspect that directly impacts on time management is illness. Busy people have a tendency to try and work despite illness. This can be bad time management. While you are ill, the quality of your work and decision making deteriorates. Your interpersonal skills weaken, because like it or not, you are thinking more about yourself than usual. It makes good time management sense to take the time off work to get better quickly, rather than soldier on and drag out an illness for weeks.

CLUTCHING AT STRAWS

When we finally realize just how much we are doing to mess up our own time, it is not uncommon to clutch at straws. To search for some sort of miracle cure that will make everything better. It might be a set of rules to obey, or an off-the-shelf time management system. None of these approaches is necessarily bad. But there are pitfalls attached. We'll look at the systems in greater detail in the next chapter. The biggest danger with a system is that it becomes a time waster in its own right. Rules are more insidious, but carry their own dangers.

THE RULES

It's an attractive proposition that there should be a set of rules for ideal time management. Just follow these seven (or 10, or 12... or whatever) prescriptions and you will change your life. It's easy (at least to specify), you can stick them on a card and laminate them, and you can have a nice, easy checklist. Done that, done that... OK, now my time is managed.

Unfortunately there are two problems with rules in this sort of circumstance. Rules are ideal for a simple, confined world. It's fine to have rules when you are playing *Monopoly*, because you know that the players will always have the same starting positions, and that no one is going to come along and totally rearrange the board into three dimensions overnight. Life very definitely ain't like that. As we've already discussed with the matter of the tidy desk syndrome, everyone is not the same and will not respond the same way to a standard rule. What's more, the world is constantly changing, thrashing about, riding a roller coaster of influences. A rule that was valuable today may be worthless tomorrow.

This being the case, is it possible to put together a book like this with a set of time management exercises? Luckily, yes. Partly because the approach is driven by principles rather than rules. Not 'have six action areas' and 'never spend more than 20 minutes on phone calls each day', but 'establish your priorities in work and private time', or 'restrict phone calls to appropriate slots in the day'. Even so, some of the exercises here will not be particularly valuable for you as an individual. Don't worry – by breaking the requirement down into a lot of small components it is possible to mix and match your ideal set of techniques.

3

MANAGING OUTSIDE INFLUENCES

IT'S ALL THEIR FAULT

We've all been in the situation. You know exactly what you are going to do today – you are going to achieve so much. There is a mountain of work and you are going to carve your way through it. Everything starts wonderfully, then 20 minutes in, the phone rings. From then on it's downhill. There are phone calls, there are personal visitors, there are e-mails. Someone wants to chat about last night's TV. Someone else wants to know about that important report that you are working on – that doesn't need to be finished for another week. Someone else wants to sell you toner cartridges. Then all hell breaks loose at the coffee machine when it swallows someone's money and the catering representative won't give a refund. All of a sudden it's lunch time, your whole morning has gone and you have achieved absolutely nothing.

Even if you have got your own time entirely under control, you can be sure that other people are going to mess up your plans. No one operates in a total vacuum, isolated from everyone else. So managing other people's impact on your time is just as important as managing your own.

HOW 'THEY' GET IN THE WAY

People have very specific ways of using up your time. A lot of it is in communication. Communication is an absolute essential for business success, yet there comes a point when it prevents you from getting something done. There is an awful lot of information out there. You only have to browse the World Wide Web for a while to realize just how much there is. Before long, you will also realize how much of it is irrelevant. As the Web is the nearest thing we have to being able to publish our individual thoughts, it's not surprising that most people are also seething with tracts of information that is of no value to you (at least, right now. Remember that timeliness is an important aspect of time management). Sadly, many of those people want to impart this useless information to you, eating up your time.

Sometimes, people can get in the way just by being there. They might not realize that they are disrupting your time management at all. Whether it's a streaker outside the office, or someone who insists on having a loud phone call standing a few feet away, you can be subject to stray cross-inputs: sights, sounds, even smells that distract.

A particular business favourite is the meeting. Meetings are almost living creatures. Once a regular meeting is established, it is hard to kill it off. Even when it ceases to have any function, it can go on eating up time, generating a whole pile of minutes and generally getting in the way. There are very few people who argue that they don't go to enough meetings. Yet the intentions of meetings are entirely laudable. They are there to enable decisions to be made, to enhance communication, to get things done. You will find meetings cropping up several times in the exercises, because they are such a prime time waster, despite being so valuable. A list of just how meetings waste time could be as long as a meeting itself. Waiting for people to arrive, not having a clear purpose, not producing any actions, talking over the same issues over and over again… you have all been there, and wished you weren't.

The final challenge 'they' can throw in your way is inappropriate tasks that there is no possibility of fitting into your schedule. This is the other end of poor delegation – the receiving end. We've all been asked to do something that will 'only take a few minutes' which has then taken all day. Most of us have also been given tasks that were incredibly urgent, pushing everything else aside, only to have the output sit on a desk unnoticed for days afterwards. Even if you work for yourself, this problem doesn't go away. There are always going to be 'them', whether they are tax inspectors, spouses or clients who can make unreasonable claims on your time.

WHY 'THEY' GET IN THE WAY

It's useful to take a moment to step back and ask why those people insist on messing up your superbly planned day. It is highly unlikely to be a matter of malice. These people are not out to wreck things, but they do have their own agendas. A common cause is simple ignorance. They didn't know you were doing something else. How could they?

Unless the people who are likely to eat up your time know your priorities, know just what you are doing and why, they have no reason not to interrupt. They've got their own priorities, they don't know yours – why shouldn't they act? On a micro level, it is very difficult to tell whether an individual is deep in thought or simply waiting for someone to come and talk to them. Unless you have clear signs of your personal state, you are bound to be interrupted.

Meetings are a more complex problem. They are ingrained into the system as a way of making things happen. Unless you start to chip away at the whole system that your company uses, meetings will continue to be a burden. Those who call a meeting aren't consciously setting out to waste time – although they may be just as unaware of your other commitments as anyone else. Once a meeting is established there's even more of a problem, as it often requires conscious effort just to stop it from continuing. The 'why' of meetings is often as much about inertia as it is about corporate structures.

Again, the evil delegator may well be unaware of your existing commitments. But there's more that can be at fault here. Where delegation involves a task that the delegator isn't qualified to do themselves, there may well be a lack of understanding of just what the task will entail, and therefore how much time it will take up. This is a surprisingly strong argument for the unfashionable view that managers should be good at the area that they manage. That the best IT (substitute a subject of your choice) managers know about IT, and are capable of doing the jobs in their area. Not as well as their best employees, but well enough to know what a task entails. In the 1980s it was popular to subscribe to the view of managers as generalists. A good manager could manage any function, they just needed to know about people. Now we're seeing a better understanding of managers as specialists. Of course this applies most in technical areas like IT, and more in middle management than top management, but the argument is strong.

DO YOU REALLY WANT TO STOP THEM?

It isn't always the case that you even want to stop others upsetting your time management. Sometimes the interruption can be entirely justified. It might be that it genuinely does take priority over what you are doing. It may be that you will benefit from a brief distraction. As demonstrated in *Instant Teamwork*, the sister book to this which covers icebreakers, warm-ups and time-outs to improve team interaction, it is often the case that you will get stuck in a rut and a brief distraction will actually result in better output rather than worse.

However, there are plenty of cases where you can be confident that you are justified in wanting to stop or modify an interruption, a meeting or an impossible delegation. The time management toolkit combines some defences to reduce the penetration of unwanted contacts, some analysis tools to find out where meetings and delegations are inappropriate, and actions to stop them without causing too much friction.

IT'S NOT JUST PEOPLE

People are not alone in their ability to capture and overwhelm your time. Just as the nearly-alive meeting can provide problems, there are other non-human contributors to your schedule. The personal computer and the network can be a huge time waster, even if each also has the potential to be extremely beneficial. Similarly, lots of other physical and non-physical (approximately hardware and software) influences can conspire to make things worse.

TECHNO TOYS

Having said that IT isn't the sole problem, it certainly can be a huge one for the susceptible. Unless IT is designed to perform a sole task – in which case it loses much of its flexibility – it is all too easy to get distracted by one of the other functions that it can perform. The most obvious example is the ability to play games on a business PC. From the first days of PCs, there have been games. Now they are extremely sophisticated, and can eat up time effortlessly and, for some, addictively.

More subtly, it is possible to spend endless hours tinkering with a computer, trying to get it past the 80 per cent level to perfection. In either case, it isn't a simple, clear-cut problem. Imposing a rule that there are no games on work PCs is not an adequate answer. It might be, for example, that someone finds that they work better if they have half an hour game break mid-afternoon. If your company can be flexible enough to allow this, it will get much better productivity out of that individual (and will be likely to keep them longer). Yet you don't want people spending all their time playing games. There's an element here that's not really about time management at all. This dilemma underlines the need to move to more measurement of output than input. Not how many hours a person spends at their computer (or desk or whatever), but what do they actually achieve. If it can be done better 'their' way, maybe there is an argument for allowing the game break. But under such circumstances the individual needs better than average time management, or they will find that their game break has taken over the whole afternoon and a vital output has been delayed.

TECHNO AIDS

Just like people, technology is not all negative when it comes to time management. There are specific products which will help with time management, from personal information managers to e-mail. The crucial test of a piece of technology is comparing the cost of setting it up and managing it with the benefits of using it. For example, an electronic diary based on your desktop PC with no remote connections is of limited use if you are always on the road.

Look out for opportunities of synergy. Gradually the makers of these products are beginning to get their act together and combine functions. For example, Microsoft's Outlook has an address book which will feed addresses to Word when writing letters, will supply fax numbers to fax software and supplies e-mail addresses to its own e-mail feature. This breadth of functionality gives significantly more benefit to balance the need to keep your electronic address book up-to-date.

ADMIN INERTIA

A particular irritating outside timewaster is administration. Most administrative systems and bureaucracy were set up with the best of intentions. Unfortunately, those intentions have usually been swamped by a reality that does not match the need that caused the systems to be set up in the first place. And systems have a life of their own, carrying on with relentless inertia long after they have outlived their usefulness.

There will almost always be administration which you undertake that is entirely unnecessary. Sometimes it will be possible to just stop doing it. You can either challenge the rules, which might result in them being changed, or in you being marked as a troublemaker, or you can bend the rules. For example, at the last large company where I worked, you had to fill out a form to request leave. Your manager then ticked off how much leave you had taken on a card, to make sure you weren't taking too much. Several of my managers took the point of view that I was trustworthy, so we did not bother with leave recording. I took time off when appropriate and no one bothered to check exactly how much I had taken. This had a double positive effect of making me feel valued by my manager and saving us the wasted time and effort of bureaucracy.

Whether you choose to challenge the need for administrative time wasting or simply cheat the system depends on your position in the company and your circumstances. If you are very senior, or your company has the sort of culture where constructive criticism is genuinely appreciated, get the bureaucracy removed. If, as is sadly often the case, yours is a company where appearances are much more important than reality, you are probably better off finding ways around the bureaucracy.

PLANES, TRAINS AND AUTOMOBILES

There's a type of outside influence on your time that is particularly insidious – travel. In part, the sneakiness of travel is its obvious requirement. No one wants to spend an hour and a half sitting in a car travelling to work, then an hour and a half travelling home again, but that's what's necessary to do the job. This is, of course, rubbish. A more accurate statement is that 'given the need to go into that particular location to do that specific job at that specific time while living where I live, and assuming I have to drive, I'm going to spend three hours a day in a car.' There are lots of possible variables there, from the assumption that you have to go into the office to do your job to the assumption that you are going to drive. Each assumption can be challenged in ways that would make more time available for other activities. Of course, the result of the challenge may be unacceptable, but that doesn't mean it's not worth examining the alternatives.

The other problem is with a different type of travel. Only a masochist could consider commuting enjoyable, but throw in plane travel to an exotic location and suddenly everyone goes ga-ga. Announce that you are having to travel halfway around the world to give a half-hour presentation and there will be lots of nudge-nudge, wink-wink 'it's a hard job, but someone's got to do it' remarks. Yet what's the reality? You are going to be stuck waiting a couple of hours at each airport, crammed into a ridiculously tight space on a plane, then spend most of your time at your destination jet-lagged and ineffective. There is nothing wrong with business travel, in fact the benefits of face-to-face communication are so huge that they often outweigh the disbenefits, but never forget what a time management nightmare such a business trip is.

SHINY SYSTEMS

Time management is a field that is awash with shiny systems. Attractive personal organizers with all sorts of sexy stationery. Special software that allows you to allocate time to the nearest minute, then track your performance. You'll find some references to these systems in Chapter 5. Feel free to try some of them out. If they work for you, great. But just like the approach to clutter on the desk, don't feel that you are a failure if time management systems leave you cold. You can manage just as well with a diary and a notebook.

The most important consideration is not to be lured into unnecessary use of systems. Remember that the vendors of paper-based systems are in business to sell paper. It's in their interests to introduce as many new and different forms as they think they can get away with selling. Now they may well have very good time management principles at heart, but think twice before buying every new piece of stationery. Similarly, the computer-based systems have a pitfall. Because computers are so good at adding and checking and monitoring, they always provide the option of inputting much more information than you really need. It's quite possible to find that your time management system is taking up too much of your time. Make sure that you are only filling in the information that is necessary.

THE BASIC REQUIREMENTS

Whether or not you go for an all-singing, all-dancing system you will need some tools to help with your time management. These might be electronic or something as simple as a notebook. There are four key requirements. A diary, both to schedule meetings and (probably more important) your own activities. A contact list – names, address, phone numbers and e-mail addresses as a bare minimum (see *We have contact* 4.39). A task list – things to do (see *Tasks, tasks* 4.25). And a general notebook (see *Nota bene* 4.50). Somewhere, for example, to keep track of your progress on some of the exercises you will be undertaking.

4

THE EXERCISES

4.1 | *Talent spotting*

Preparation None.
Running time Five minutes.
Resources None.
Timescale Annual.

Time for some self-assessment. Run through the activities you undertake, both at work and in your social life. Trying not to be modest, what do you do well? What have you had positive feedback about? Put together a list of one-liners on your talents. Don't separate work and social: they are all talents.

Now extend out along the timeline. What did you do years ago that you were good at, but haven't done since? Also, think yourself into the future. Is there anything that you've never actually done, but think you would be good at? This is not a matter of impossible dreams, but talents you feel you may well have, given the chance.

It might be necessary to do a second cut at your list, combining similar items that have arisen from different sources.

Feedback   The point of time management is to ensure that more time is available for the things you really want to do. One of the useful starting points is the talents you can bring to play. It may be that some of your talents appear useless, there may be things you are good at but hate – it doesn't matter, it's still worth establishing what they are.

Outcome   Out of this exercise you should get a one page talent list. We will use this as input to various other exercises – keep it somewhere easily accessed, whether it's in an appropriate folder on your PC, in your personal organizer, or in a particular file (or pile) in your system.

Variations   There isn't much variation here. It's probably best to revisit your talents annually, or after a burst of training, but they usually change quite slowly, so it isn't the end of the world if you don't polish them too often. Like anything that is only updated irregularly, your talent list is easy to forget. Why not put an entry in your schedule to revisit it?

Managing yourself	❂❂❂❂
Managing other people	❂
Managing externals	❂
Business impact	❂❂❂❂
Social impact	❂❂❂❂
Fun	❂❂❂

4.2 | *If I were a rich man*

Preparation None.
Running time Five minutes.
Resources None.
Timescale Annual.

The first step to time management isn't getting a diary or scheduling tasks, it's finding out what you want to do with your time. This exercise helps to establish your desires. Imagine you have come into a huge sum of money. You will never have to work again. Take a minute to enjoy the thought and its immediate implications.

Now jot down the main activities you undertake – between 10 and 20. Don't differentiate between work and social activities – list everything significant. Then draw up three columns: 'Yes', 'No' and 'New'. Assign all your activities to one of the first two columns. What would you do anyway? What would you instantly dismiss?

With the first two columns filled in, consider the third. It would be helpful to have completed the *Talent spotting* (4.1) exercise before doing this. Given the freedom provided by your riches, what else would you do? Try to be realistic, considering your talents, but be happy to stretch yourself.

Feedback Don't skip this and others early exercises because they seem 'wishy-washy'. They are essential. Without this step, the reasoning behind choosing your focal activities and allocating your time is missing.

Outcome The outcome of the first few exercises in the book is a clearer understanding of what you want to do with your time.

Variations Personal goals change, although often slowly. What you wanted to do while at school will often be very different to your feelings after a few years in a job. Having a family, changing careers, redundancy – plenty of outside forces alter your needs, as do internal pressures like the mid-life crisis. You should refresh this list when you hit such a milestone. You may want to revisit it annually – New Year or a birthday is a good point. To make sure it happens, put it in your diary.

Managing yourself	✪✪✪✪
Managing other people	✪✪
Managing externals	✪✪
Business impact	✪✪✪✪
Social impact	✪✪✪✪
Fun	✪✪✪✪

4.3 | *Dream day*

Preparation None.
Running time Five minutes.
Resources None.
Timescale One-off.

Along with the other activities at the start of the chapter, *Dream day* helps clarify what you want to do with your time. Without this knowledge, there is little point in developing skills at using time better, because there is no yardstick by which to measure 'better'.

Make sure you are relaxed. Find an armchair in a quiet setting. Get a cup of coffee. Play some music that helps you to unwind. Now put together a schedule for a dream of a day. In detail (including, for instance, what you do between waking up and getting dressed), map out exactly what you would do if you had a whole 24 hours with total control over your time.

Now pick out the activities that you want to carry forward. You may have to modify an unreachable dream to become practical (if stretching) – still, make sure that the key aspects of your dream day are reflected in your output.

Feedback Resist the urge to censor. After extracting the useful cues, you can bin the output. So if your dream day involves a jacuzzi with a film star or shooting next door's cat, don't worry – get it down, then think about the practical goals you can deduce.

Outcome This exercise is useful in combination with *If I were a rich man* (4.2) to round out your dream goals.

Variations There are other ways to tease out desires. If your mind works well with categories, break down what you would like to do into categories, and subcategories and so on (a mind map works well). Think what you would do if you were stranded on a desert island with plenty of physical resources and lots of time. Or locked in a shopping mall for a weekend with all the contents of the mall available to you. Try using different slants to widen your picture of your personal goals.

Managing yourself	✪✪✪✪
Managing other people	✪
Managing externals	✪
Business impact	✪✪✪✪
Social impact	✪✪✪✪
Fun	✪✪✪

4.4 | *Obstacle map*

Preparation Personal goals.
Running time Five minutes.
Resources Notebook.
Timescale Annual.

Before performing this exercise, try some of the earlier ones to establish your personal goals. This exercise will help where you have a goal, but not a clear way of achieving it. If you don't have problems like this, you don't need this exercise – but you will be unusual. Take a goal from the earlier exercises – a way you want to change your life, or just something you want to do. If it isn't obvious how to achieve your goal, try this exercise. First note what the goal is. Jot down a few short phrases identifying not just what you want, but what it implies, what surrounds the goal.

Now make a few one-line notes summarizing your starting point. What is different from your goal? What would have to change? Finally, fill in the obstacles that are preventing you from moving immediately to your goal state. What is lacking? What is getting in the way? Sometimes the obstacles will be the starting point itself – don't worry, still list them.

Feedback If there weren't obstacles, your goals would have already been achieved. Explicitly identifying the obstacles is very valuable because often you are so focused on where you are now, or where you want to go, that you don't consider what's in the way.

Outcome The result of this exercise is to generate a new set of goals, overcoming the obstacles you have identified. For example, if a goal was 'to run my own courier business', one obstacle might be 'no employees' – so a new goal might be 'recruit appropriate employees'.

Variations You might find this technique easier if you use a large sheet of paper turned sideways. Draw three boxes, from left to right: starting point, obstacles and goal. Using this structure may help you to visualize what is going on. Resist any inclination to jump straight to the obstacles: the sequence of goal, then starting point, then obstacles is essential.

Managing yourself	○○○○
Managing other people	○○
Managing externals	○○
Business impact	○○○○
Social impact	○○○○
Fun	○○

4.5 | *What's it worth?*

Preparation Some of the earlier exercises.
Running time Five minutes.
Resources Notebook.
Timescale One-off.

This is an exercise to undertake when you have a reasonably clear picture of your personal goals. The first exercises in the chapter develop these – if you haven't done any yet, try a couple. Start with a list of these goals on a piece of paper – don't try to keep them in your head.

Put four columns alongside your goals: cash, thrill, leverage and availability. Give each goal a rating in the first three columns. Cash should indicate direct earnings. Thrill should show how much of a buzz you will get out of achieving the goal. Leverage indicates how much achieving this goal can support other goals. Rate them as accurately as you can. For example, try to put figures in the cash column rather than 'low' or 'high'.

Finally fill in the availability column, indicating whether the chances of achieving the goal are low or high, and whether this is likely to be a one-off source, or continuing.

Feedback Without knowing how you value your goals, it is hard to allocate time to them. For example, writing a book usually scores low on cash. In fact, for many authors, it's on a par with working in a hamburger restaurant. Yet the activity often scores high on thrill, and has considerable potential to support other goals like consultancy. Too often we only consider the cash dimension – having a value list helps to ensure that we don't fall into that trap.

Outcome This exercise explores the relative values of the activities and goals that you aspire to. It isn't possible to simply prioritize these goals, but these values should give you a better idea of the balance you need to achieve.

Variations You may wish reassess your values when reassessing your personal goals. See the Variations section of *If I were a rich man* (4.2).

Managing yourself	✪✪✪✪
Managing other people	✪✪
Managing externals	✪✪
Business impact	✪✪✪✪
Social impact	✪✪✪✪
Fun	✪✪✪

4.6 | *Where'd it go?*

Preparation None.
Running time Five minutes.
Resources Diary; paper.
Timescale One-off.

It is often difficult to appreciate just where your time has gone. Look back over the last typical week you had. Your diary will probably help. Starting with the 168 hours you have in the week, allocate each to one of a number of headings. Try: sleep, paid work, social, maintenance (both self and belongings), unpaid work and study. You should be able to fit all your activities into these headings without too much trouble.

Now have a look at how that time balances out – a bar chart is a good way of getting an overview of the implications. How do you feel about the relative times you spend on your different activities? We aren't going to do anything actively with this data right now, but it will be an important input to the decisions you will be making. In *How long?* (4.41) we will look at achieving a better balance between work and social, but the purpose of this exercise is to understand your position.

Feedback Good time management is all about balance. Remember there isn't any wasted time, just time that is used more or less effectively for your purposes.

Outcome Without a reasonable feeling for where your time is going now, you are unlikely to have a good idea of the balance and the need for change. Although this exercise doesn't result in immediate action, it will give you an essential picture of your starting point.

Variations The best way to put together a summary like this is to keep a log for a week, noting as you do it which category your activity fits into. Not many people do this as it seems too much hassle. It's a pity, because without a log it is very difficult to be realistic about the way you spend your time, and keeping one for a week is very little burden. Give it a try.

Managing yourself	✪✪✪✪
Managing other people	✪✪✪✪
Managing externals	✪✪✪
Business impact	✪✪✪✪
Social impact	✪✪
Fun	✪✪

4.7 | *Hot spots*

Preparation None.
Running time Five minutes.
Resources Paper and two coloured pens.
Timescale One-off.

No one functions at top efficiency all the time. There will be certain times of day when you work particularly well or particularly poorly.

Turn a sheet of paper sideways. Draw three parallel lines across it. Label the top 'high', the next 'medium' and the bottom 'low'. List hours along the bottom, from your typical waking time to your typical bedtime. Think through your day. When are the times (typically two or three a day) that you are most effective? Using the second colour, draw a bar along the top line for each of these periods. Now think when you are particularly sluggish and unresponsive. Again there will typically be two or three periods. Highlight these on the bottom line. Fill in the remainder of the day on the middle line, then join the segments with vertical lines, so you have a chart of your personal energy levels.

Feedback When planning activities, try to fit in with your time graph. High times are best for developing new ideas, key meetings, creativity, etc. Medium times are best for everyday work, non-essential communication and meetings, and reading which requires concentration. Low times should be reserved for the humdrum – administration, reading requiring little concentration, and so forth. Keep your time chart easily visible so you can refer to it throughout the day. When you have no choice about timing, be aware of the need to make extra effort when your energy is low.

Outcome If you use your time chart when booking meetings and deciding what tasks you take on, you will find that you get the best results for high energy activities, and make best use of your less productive times. What's more you feel much less sense of frustration.

Variations If you have clear variations on cycles other than the day, you might produce a chart for these also, but usually the daily variation is the strongest.

Managing yourself	✪✪✪✪
Managing other people	✪
Managing externals	✪
Business impact	✪✪✪
Social impact	✪✪✪
Fun	✪✪

4.8 | *Focus*

Preparation Talents/desires exercises.
Running time 10 minutes.
Resources Notebook.
Timescale Monthly.

A fundamental assumption of time management is that you allocate time to things you really want to do. In other activities, such as *Talent spotting* (4.1) you have the opportunity to identify your abilities and desires. If you haven't tried the first four exercises yet, it is worth doing so before continuing.

Look through your talents and personal goals. The aim is to pull together a handful of focal activities. Sometimes called key areas, these form the core of what you do, both at work and socially. There should be at least four of these and not more than eight. Beyond this they become unmanageable. Don't go into detail. Focal activities can have an end-point in mind, but shouldn't be specific tasks. So, for instance, a focal activity could be 'improve my tennis' or 'launch a new product by next Spring', but not 'buy a new racket' or 'arrange for advertising'.

Feedback You may find it is difficult to pinpoint your focal activities. Take a first shot, and if you find important aspects of your life aren't covered, rearrange them. If you are worried about missing detail, you will find more in *Chunking* (4.13), *The top 10 list* (4.10) and *Tasks, tasks* (4.25). If you have lots of focal activities, you will lack direction. Ruthlessly select the most important seven or eight. Just because an activity isn't listed, it doesn't mean that it won't get done, just that it isn't fundamental.

Outcome Without focus you cannot sensibly allocate your time, and you are unlikely to complete major projects and activities. This is one of the most important exercises in the book.

Variations Your focal activities need revisiting at least annually, but for many a monthly review is more appropriate. It need not be a lengthy exercise, taking no more than five minutes. However, like all regular, infrequent tasks, it ought to be scheduled.

Managing yourself	○○○○
Managing other people	○○
Managing externals	○○
Business impact	○○○○
Social impact	○○○○
Fun	○○

4.9 | *The e-mail of the species*

Preparation None.
Running time Five minutes.
Resources E-mail software.
Timescale Ongoing.

E-mail has revolutionized business communications and is making rapid inroads into the social world. However, it comes with a price. Reading and responding to e-mail takes time, and the immediacy can provide a constant distraction. Keeping e-mail in its place is a three-stage process.

Firstly, turn off notification. Stop your e-mail package from telling you when e-mail arrives. Secondly, have between one and four e-mail slots in your schedule. These needn't be explicitly in your diary, although it may help. They should be the only times you read e-mail. (This doesn't mean they are the only times to send e-mail – check *Offloading ideas* (4.18) to see how sending e-mails instantly can benefit you.)

Finally, be brutal about time. Fix a maximum time – perhaps 30 minutes, certainly no more than an hour – to spend on e-mails. Stick to this by skimming through your in-tray first, reading key messages and responding, then working through low priority mail. Don't feel you have to read all of a low priority message: bin it as soon as you are sure it's irrelevant. Whatever you do, don't let unread mail build up in your in-tray. Similarly, if you have to reply, try to do so immediately.

Feedback Have a standard 'sorry I haven't time' (or 'no thanks') message for unimportant e-mails requiring a reply. If the sender doesn't get anything, they may keep re-sending the mail. This isn't helpful to anyone.

Outcome Freedom from notification is a big relief. Once you see a mail has arrived, it will continue to nag. Is it important? Who is it from? It's much better not to know it has arrived. By managing e-mail reading into sensible chunks it remains a valuable resource, but won't take over your life.

Variations Consider using mail filters to organize incoming mail, see *Filter tips* (4.57). If you have a hot spots chart, see *Hot Spots* (4.7), fit e-mail reading into lower energy times.

Managing yourself	❂❂❂
Managing other people	❂❂❂❂
Managing externals	❂❂❂❂
Business impact	❂❂❂❂
Social impact	❂❂
Fun	❂❂

4.10 | *The top 10 list*

Preparation None.
Running time Five minutes.
Resources None.
Timescale Weekly.

Note your top 10 concerns for the coming week. If you have already done the *Focus* exercise (4.8), many of these concerns will be driven by your focal activities. Put the list somewhere very visible. If you have staff, e-mail them a copy.

Whenever you start a task, glance at the top 10 list. Does the task influence your top 10? If it doesn't, you may still do it, but bear in mind its relative unimportance. If you are asked to do something which doesn't fit with your list and you are short of time, say 'no'. Find it difficult? See *Why not no?* (4.12) and *No, I can* (4.19). Next week, when you draw up your list, make sure there are changes. There may be ongoing priorities, but if everything stays the same from week to week you are stagnating.

Feedback This is a good exercise to start early because it can stand alone.

Outcome The top 10 list cuts through your potential activities to the essentials. It's great both for work and at home. I was introduced to the idea of sharing your list with staff by Nick Spooner, MD of Internet commerce company Entranet. Nick used his top 10 list to communicate priorities to his staff – before long they all had their own lists in public view. This has significantly improved the company's effectiveness. A side effect of the top 10 list is to reduce irrelevant interruptions. A meaningful look at the list as someone comes close can cause them to reassess their priorities.

Variations It may be necessary to have several lists. For example, top 10 customers and top 10 milestones. The actual subjects need to be matched to your line of business, but don't be tempted to have more than two or three – you need to be able to take in the lists at a glance.

Managing yourself	✪✪✪✪
Managing other people	✪✪✪✪
Managing externals	✪
Business impact	✪✪✪✪
Social impact	✪✪✪
Fun	✪✪

4.11 | *Scrap the briefcase*

Preparation None.
Running time 10 minutes.
Resources Briefcase.
Timescale One-off.

Compartmentalization is essential for good time management. Being able to slice off a chunk of a task, get it done, then switch attention elsewhere. Nowhere is this more essential than in the division between business and social life. It's accepted that we shouldn't allow social life to intrude too far into work, yet the reverse is rarely true. This exercise involves setting up a beachhead against intrusion. In another exercise – *Banning homework* (4.71) – we will build on the achievement.

If you haven't got a briefcase (or other means of carrying documents home), skip straight onto *Banning homework*. Otherwise, open that briefcase up. See what you carry around. How much of the contents make several trips to and from home? Keep an eye on it over a week. See how much you use it, and what for.

Now substitute a bag that is more appropriate for your specific needs. For instance, a shoulder bag is better if you have to carry any weight. Or a carrier bag might be better for your sandwiches. Whatever the requirement, make sure you change to a very different bag. Prompted by the new bag, be conscious of putting things into it. Beyond basics like a pen, only put something in if you are going to use it that day.

Feedback   This isn't about reducing the weight you carry around, it's about a change of attitude.

Outcome   This exercise is the first step to making an effective division between business and social time. It also helps to ensure the right priorities are given to documents.

Variations   It's sometimes difficult to be honest. You put some papers in to read tonight, then there are better things to do and the papers stay there for days. Try this: each morning, throw away anything in your briefcase without an action attached. Too drastic? Okay, put anything that isn't read the night you take it home on your desk – but it's nowhere near as effective.

Managing yourself	❍❍❍
Managing other people	❍
Managing externals	❍❍❍❍
Business impact	❍❍❍
Social impact	❍❍❍
Fun	❍❍❍

4.12 | *Why not no?*

Preparation None.
Running time Five minutes.
Resources Diary.
Timescale One-off.

There are few more powerful time management tools than being able to say 'no'. It's a difficult thing to do, though, partly because we want to be polite and partly because we don't want to miss out, whether it's on some fun, some payment or a chance to improve our image.

This is a two stage technique, which is completed in *No, I can* (4.19). The first step is understanding why you say 'no'. Take a couple of minutes thinking through your own response to being asked to do something. Why don't you say 'no' more often?

Now spend a couple of minutes looking at recent appointments in your diary, and thinking through the tasks you have taken on in the last week or so. Are there meetings you have attended or work you've done (include leisure activities) which hadn't got a high value output to you or your family or your company? Why didn't you say 'no'? Make two short lists – things I take on unnecessarily and why I don't say 'no'.

Feedback   Keep these lists to one side for the second saying 'no' activity. Meanwhile, when you take on new tasks and appointments, bear them in mind. You needn't act yet (although feel free to if you want to), but be aware of what you are doing.

Outcome   Finding out why you don't say 'no' more is an essential step on the road to controlling when you want to reject. Simply being aware of what you are doing is often enough to make a significant change to your behaviour.

Variations   Alternatives for exploring why you don't say 'no' are thinking about the people you interact with (business and social) and why you don't say 'no' to them, and thinking about the ways you get involved in something – face-to-face request, letter, e-mail, recurring meeting, etc.

Managing yourself	✪✪✪✪
Managing other people	✪✪✪✪
Managing externals	✪
Business impact	✪✪✪✪
Social impact	✪✪✪✪
Fun	✪✪

4.13 | *Chunking*

Preparation *Focus* exercise (4.8).
Running time Five minutes.
Resources Notebook.
Timescale Weekly.

We all have activities that can't be completed in a single session, day or even year. This is true of most focal activities, see *Focus* (4.8) – they need to be broken down into manageable chunks. This is a fundamental part of good time management (and why the style of this book is so appropriate). Take each focal activity and break it into segments or tasks. Each task should have a clear outcome and completion date. It doesn't matter whether or not the activity has an end date – the chunks should have clear timing. For example, taking the two example activities in *Focus*, 'improve my tennis' might include 'start tennis lessons by 1st March' and 'buy a new racquet by 14th March'. Similarly 'launch a new product by next Spring' might have tasks like 'hold idea generation sessions by 1st October', 'select and polish product concept by 18th October'.

Feedback   It is important that you set dates and deliverables, but remember that the dates are guesswork. Your task list should be revised weekly, throwing off completed tasks, reassessing dates and adding new ones. For more nitty-gritty detail on chunking, see *Tasks, tasks* (4.25).

Outcome   It is a mistake that is often made to think that good time management consists only of focus and chunking. Without the awareness of your personal priorities they are useless – but based on priorities they are an essential component.

Variations   You may need more detail. Some chunks might be broken into sub-chunks. A task may involve others, so you may need to indicate who is involved and get their feedback. Electronic time management products often allow you to allocate tasks to others, then capture the results. This is fine as long as maintenance of task information doesn't become a major task in its own right. If you have a long list of tasks, you will need to bring in *Priorities* (4.16).

Managing yourself	✪✪✪✪
Managing other people	✪✪
Managing externals	✪✪
Business impact	✪✪✪✪
Social impact	✪✪✪✪
Fun	✪✪

4.14 | *Calling by numbers*

Preparation None.
Running time Five minutes.
Resources Telephone.
Timescale Daily.

Most days you will make phone calls. Some are known about in advance, others crop up throughout the day. This technique reduces the tendency of outgoing calls to fragment your activities. You'll find more on incoming calls in *Telephone tag* (4.23) and *Whosat?* (4.66).

Where much time management is about breaking activities down, this is about chunking up, pulling together small tasks that would otherwise waste time. In a business context, you can normally restrict outgoing calls to two chunks, mid-morning and mid-afternoon. This reduces time wasting, and maximizes the chance of a reply by using core business hours. Making it happen is simply a matter of keeping a call list. At the start of the day, put any planned calls on the list. As the need arises, add new items – don't be tempted to make the call unless timing is critical.

Feedback   There will be exceptions – good time management is about principles, not rules – but most calls can be handled this way.

Outcome   This technique cuts interruptions to your work flow, and maximizes the chance of getting through first time. For those who dislike using the phone, it also minimizes the pain and forces the issue – it's easier to put off an individual call than a list.

Variations   Some personal information manager software lets you build a call list that dials automatically – so much the better. Make sure the list is in a single place. If you have a 'mess of paper' system, keep to a single sheet – yellow sticky notes are too easy to misplace. On hearing an engaged tone, press 5 (or equivalent) to get an automatic callback when the number is free. This won't work with all exchanges, but is very effective if it does. If you have callbacks outstanding when the period is over, cancel them, making sure the individual is still on your call list.

Managing yourself	✪✪✪✪
Managing other people	✪✪✪
Managing externals	✪✪✪
Business impact	✪✪✪✪
Social impact	✪✪
Fun	✪✪

4.15 | *Quiet corners*

Preparation None.
Running time Five minutes.
Resources None.
Timescale Ongoing.

Getting on with something that needs your full attention is impossible if you are constantly interrupted. Consider hunting out a quiet corner. Thanks to laptop computers, many more work activities can now be done away from the desk. Even without a laptop, you can use that classic mobile solution, a pad and paper.

Where you get to depends on you and your environment. If your workplace has hot desking, or guest worker spaces, try finding a space in a different part of the building. If there are small meeting rooms, book one for a meeting with yourself. Quite often on a large site there will be unoccupied offices. Take one over for the afternoon.

If none of these is practical, there are quiet corners that you can subvert. If your company has a library or management study centre, try hiding there. Alternatively, venture out into the world, to a public library or even (weather and location permitting) a field or a beach.

Feedback Bear in mind the need to be perceived as hard working as well as actually being hard working (see Chapter 1, page 7). Leaving the company site would only work with a flexible employer (or if you are relatively senior). If it is likely to be a problem, make sure that there is a prominent notice on your desk saying that you are in a meeting, and when you will be back.

Outcome Finding a quiet retreat is increasingly important in a world where communications and open plan open us up to constant interruption. If it shows signs of becoming a way of life, work hard on something like working from home – see *Home, sweet home* (4.48); otherwise it's a great way of protecting a time slot for productive work.

Variations There is no point seeking out a quiet corner if you take your mobile phone, your pager and wireless e-mail. Turn them off or leave them behind.

Managing yourself	❂❂❂
Managing other people	❂❂❂❂
Managing externals	❂❂❂❂
Business impact	❂❂❂❂
Social impact	❂❂
Fun	❂❂❂

4.16 | *Priorities*

Preparation *Chunking* exercise (4.13).
Running time Five minutes.
Resources Notebook.
Timescale Weekly.

It isn't essential to complete *Chunking* first, but you do need a task list. Usually there is too much to do: you need priorities. A first step is to work backwards from the completion date. If a task has to be finished by the end of March and takes a day to complete, it is low priority in December. Similarly, a task with an immovable deadline tomorrow comes higher up the list. However, important though timeliness is, it isn't the prime concern. Having established the low priority of distant tasks, top priority goes to tasks that are essential to achieving your focal activities. This may mean putting off an urgent but unimportant task to make sure that a focal activity is advanced.

A final consideration is knock-on. When you have a tightly timed series of tasks and the first over-runs, what do you do? Assuming it was right to overrun, it may be worth sacrificing the next task to keep the others on schedule, rather than have everything run late.

Feedback   *Priorities* is valuable for tasks, but less practical for focal activities, see *Focus* (4.8). How do you balance, for example, improving your tennis, getting a new product to market, improving staff morale and having fun at home? Sometimes you have to do this (and work wins too often), but it shouldn't be the norm. A more useful approach is a value list – see *What's it worth?* (4.5).

Outcome   Prioritization is essential to getting the right tasks done: it's as simple as that.

Variations   You will see different approaches to prioritization in *The top 10 list* (4.10) and *Drawn and quartered* (4.67). A top 10 is complimentary. Prioritization is essential when sorting out your schedule; The *top 10 list* is better for communicating to the rest of the world, and for making on-the-spot schedule changes. *Drawn and quartered* is more similar to *Priorities*, but comes from a different direction.

Managing yourself	✪✪✪✪
Managing other people	✪✪
Managing externals	✪✪
Business impact	✪✪✪✪
Social impact	✪✪✪✪
Fun	✪✪

4.17 | *Meet yourself half way*

Preparation Have a diary.
Running time Two minutes.
Resources None.
Timescale Weekly.

Open your diary and look through this week. There will be meetings and special events. And there will probably be gaps, when you intend to get things done. Now imagine that you get a phone call. Someone asks 'What are you doing tomorrow afternoon?' 'I've nothing on,' you reply. So in goes another meeting. Unconsciously you have said that the meeting, even if it was the paper recycling committee, was more important than any other work you might do. It's horribly easy for scheduled events to hog your time.

There's only one answer; you've got to schedule meetings with yourself. Don't say this is what you are doing – it sounds terrible – but it's what you need. Each week, block off some slots. You might like a short slot each morning for admin – see *Scheduling admin* (4.37) – communications slots for e-mail and calls, and most of all, production slots to get things done. When you put a meeting in, be aware that you are cancelling something else, not putting it into free time.

Feedback   Using this technique requires a modicum of cheek. But remember, there is no deception involved; you are simply making sure that things are arranged according to your priorities. If you have trouble remembering to undertake weekly exercises like this, consider a recurring start-the-week event of carving up your diary.

Outcome   This is a powerful technique that is essential if you suffer from too many meetings. It isn't right to give meetings the priority we do. By putting other activities in your schedule, you can achieve a better balance.

Variations   A weekly approach suits most people, but you may find you need to look further ahead. Consider taking this approach with your personal time, too. You can be much more broad brush, but slotting in some time for personal projects can help to avoid them being subsumed by never-ending domestic chores.

Managing yourself	✪✪✪✪
Managing other people	✪✪✪✪
Managing externals	✪✪
Business impact	✪✪✪✪
Social impact	✪✪✪
Fun	✪✪

4.18 | *Offloading ideas*

Preparation None.
Running time Two minutes.
Resources E-mail.
Timescale Ongoing.

The brain is a wonderful thing, but it has its limitations. Just as computer programs sometimes fail to run because there aren't enough resources on the PC, our efficiency of thinking degrades as we try to juggle more and more things in our head. A classic example is during meetings, where it is all too easy to dedicate so many resources to your next contribution that you don't listen to anyone else.

The answer is to offload, freeing up valuable resources. In a meeting, it's usually a matter of jotting down your point on a pad. But a great way to free up resources when an idea or need for action suddenly hits at your desk is e-mail. Don't squirrel the idea away, it will just slow you down. Pop up the e-mail, send off a brief note, and it's gone. Out of sight, out of mind, no nagging worry. If the idea is a task for yourself, you may prefer to pop it into your task list or diary.

Feedback If you aren't at your desk, you can still use this technique as long as you've a laptop with 'store and forward' e-mail (ie, it hangs on to the mail until you are next connected), or you are near someone else's PC.

Outcome Distraction by the attempt to remember ideas and actions is a real problem, reducing quality of output and making things take longer. This technique is simple and effective.

Variations If you haven't got e-mail, you ought to have! Failing that, you could use a secretary, a notebook or a tape recorder to capture ideas, but none of these is as effective at freeing up mental resources. Don't make a note on a yellow sticky and put it somewhere obvious – this reinforces the problem. A neat trick if you are away from your desk is to borrow a PC and send yourself an e-mail.

Managing yourself	✪✪✪✪
Managing other people	✪
Managing externals	✪
Business impact	✪✪✪✪
Social impact	✪✪✪
Fun	✪✪

4.19 | *No, I can*

Preparation *Why not no?* (4.12)
Running time 10 minutes.
Resources Diary.
Timescale One-off.

This activity follows on from *Why not no?* (4.12). First look at your reasons for not saying 'no'. For each one, think of at least two counter reasons for saying 'no'. For instance, if your argument was 'because I might offend the person', counter arguments might be 'if I don't say no, I'll offend someone else' or 'I don't mind offending them'.

Now look at the things that you probably don't need to do. For each draw up a short set of pros and cons for undertaking the task. What do you get out of it? What does the company/family get out of it? What will happen if you don't do it? Why should you not do it? Who else could do it? Put a summary of what you have discovered somewhere readily visible. Next time you get a request, measure the activity against your summary. If it's covered, unless there is a strong argument for it, say 'no'. With practice it becomes easier.

Feedback There's a common misconception that saying 'no' is rude. But you aren't helping by saying 'yes', then not delivering. Try to say 'no' with a helpful suggestion and a reason. For example, 'Sorry, I can't do that for you because I'm finishing this report for the boss. Have you tried Lucy?'

Outcome Overdo saying 'no' and you will labelled unhelpful. But going too far the other way is equally dangerous. Say 'no' the right way and people will still think of you positively, but they won't impose.

Variations Don't prevaricate. 'I'll think about it' might be easier, but it's damaging both to yourself and to the person asking for help. If you are having difficulty saying 'no', try counter-loading. Say 'yes, but you'll have to help me by doing X, Y and Z' where they are the tasks you would have been doing otherwise.

Managing yourself	✪✪✪✪
Managing other people	✪✪✪✪
Managing externals	✪
Business impact	✪✪✪✪
Social impact	✪✪✪✪
Fun	✪✪

4.20 | No action, no report

Preparation None.
Running time Five minutes.
Resources For people with staff.
Timescale Ongoing.

Reports waste a lot of time. It takes time to generate them. It takes time to read them. All too often, they are an exercise in generating output that no one really wants. This exercise requires you to be slightly despotic, but in a good cause.

Put out an edict to your staff. From now on, no report is to be generated without associated actions. If they can't think of actions that are required as a result of the report being generated, it isn't to be produced. There are obvious exceptions where reports are required for legal reasons – even then, an attempt should be made to add actions.

Feedback   The whole point of producing reports is to generate action. Otherwise they're a huge waste of time and money. If it seems impossible in your particular department, I'd like to point out that this was a tip passed on to me by Brian Thomas, Finance Director of financial services giant Allied Dunbar. If a finance department, the ultimate report junkies, could operate such a scheme, so can any department.

Outcome   There is an immense feeling of relief when unnecessary reports are no longer generated, both for those who have to produce them, and for those who feel the need to look at them even if they are meaningless. This is a real all-round winner. If you feel a report does generate actions, but actions for someone else, they ought to be discussed with that someone else. That way, there will be more consensus between issuers and recipients after the event.

Variations   If you are reasonably senior in your company, consider expanding this outside your particular department. When you receive reports from elsewhere without actions, send them back immediately with a covering note explaining that they have not been read, and will not unless they come back with appropriate action points.

Managing yourself	❍❍❍
Managing other people	❍❍❍❍
Managing externals	❍❍
Business impact	❍❍❍❍
Social impact	❍
Fun	❍❍

4.21 | *A personal project*

Preparation None.
Running time 10 minutes.
Resources Output from personal goal sessions, notebook.
Timescale Annual.

Time management is as much about your home life as your business day, but most people put work first. This exercise encourages you to widen your view. The aim is to establish a new personal project – an activity towards a goal outside work that isn't currently under way. However busy you are, this is worthwhile.

Take a couple of minutes to consider anything you have on goals and skills, values and obstacles (if you don't have anything, try one or two of the first five exercises in this chapter). Identify an activity in your personal life that isn't happening or isn't being handled very well. Ideally it should be an activity that can be brought to a conclusion in a reasonable timescale – no more than six months. Now feed this activity into your plans. Make it a focal activity, see *Focus* (4.8) for more on this. Ensure that you do something on it every week, perhaps only a few minutes, but keep it alive. Now at least one personal project has made it into your priorities.

Feedback Resist the temptation to push this activity aside when time gets tight. You needn't spend long on it, but make sure it gets something weekly.

Outcome By forcing a goal outside work into your focal activities you are helping to even out the balance most of us have got drastically wrong.

Variations It's just possible that your balance is so far the other way that you have to use this exercise to get another work topic into your focal activities, but that is rare. Don't add several activities at once. Get one up and running and then consider more. Don't drop anything to add this first one. As you change the balance further you will need to, but for one new activity there should not be a need to drop anything.

Managing yourself	❍❍❍❍
Managing other people	❍
Managing externals	❍❍
Business impact	❍❍
Social impact	❍❍❍❍
Fun	❍❍❍❍

4.22 | *Travel times*

Preparation None.
Running time Five minutes.
Resources None.
Timescale One-off.

We spend a considerable amount of time travelling, much of it unproductive. Think about your travel patterns. Start with a typical week. What journeys do you make regularly? For each journey type, jot down an idea of the duration, what you can do during the journey, the purpose and the frequency.

Now think wider. Are there one-off journeys that fit a regular pattern? Perhaps attending conferences or travelling abroad to see customers. Check your journey list against your focal activities, see *Focus* (4.8). How many journeys are direct contributors to a focal activity? For example, a bus driver's journey is part of a focal activity, but the bus passengers don't actually want to travel on the bus, just to be somewhere else. How much time in a week would you free up if you could do away with travel? How much in a month?

Feedback This exercise tells you how much time you are wasting, but not how to fix it. The fix is non-trivial. For example, you can cut commuting time by working from home, changing jobs, moving house – but these are significant activities in their own right.

Outcome A better understanding of the time you spend travelling. You should then be able to take a more reasonable view when, for example, asked to travel half way around the world to attend a conference. You don't have to reject the offer, but make sure that there are enough positive contributions to your focal activities to make up for the wasted time. The exercise also provides the starting point for personal projects to reduce commuting time.

Variations If you are having trouble describing a typical travelling week, think of the different modes of travel you might use – foot, car, bus, train, plane – and the time you spend on them in a week. When you must travel, think how books on tape and other inputs could make the time more productive.

Managing yourself	❍❍❍
Managing other people	❍
Managing externals	❍❍❍❍
Business impact	❍❍❍
Social impact	❍❍
Fun	❍

4.23 | *Telephone tag*

Preparation None.
Running time Five minutes.
Resources Telephone.
Timescale Ongoing.

The telephone is powerful but intrusive. Unlike mail, phones demand attention. You can be repeatedly interrupted in the middle of an important piece of work, breaking the flow. We've all had days like this.

The most common solutions are problems themselves: having someone else answer your phone, or keeping voice mail switched on all the time. The latter gives you a reputation for never being there. The former makes you seem unapproachable. Instead, try answering your own calls part of the day. If you have a regular schedule, you could make it a specific time – perhaps answering in the afternoon. Whatever, get someone else (or voice mail) to answer your phone while you have blocked off time for work – but for at least one third, and preferably a half a day, pick up the calls.

Callers should be told that you are in a meeting, and when you will next receive calls – but also invite them to leave a message and ensure that they get a call back by the next working day.

Feedback   I have seen this approach used successfully by directors of corporates. People are initially stunned when a director answers. Strangely, the number of calls sometimes declines as some people get flustered talking to a senior person. There is nothing worse, though, than having the reputation of hiding behind voice mail. After a while people get the message. You aren't interested in them. So they don't talk to you – and you are out of the loop.

Outcome   Handling the telephone is not easy, especially if your phone system rings even if the voice mail is going to answer. But working this way will enhance your time management without degrading your image.

Variations   You could have a whole day without taking calls, but most people find it difficult to spend a whole day in solid productive concentration and benefit from occasional communication.

Managing yourself	✪✪✪
Managing other people	✪✪✪✪
Managing externals	✪✪
Business impact	✪✪✪✪
Social impact	✪✪
Fun	✪✪

4.24 | *Agenda bender*

Preparation Must be performed in advance.
Running time Two minutes.
Resources Meeting; notebook.
Timescale Ongoing.

Without agendas it is easy to hold a meeting without a clear purpose, and it is possible to spend a long time discussing irrelevant matters. Try this exercise with the next meeting you organize. First, ensure that the agenda goes out at least a week in advance. If this is not possible because of short notice, at least get the agenda out with the invitation. Next, ensure that the agenda is clear. Don't use unnecessary jargon, and make each item action oriented with a time allocation. A bad agenda item might be: 'BSC', made slightly better as 'Balanced Score Card' and much better as 'Deciding if the Balanced Score Card should be used by Finance division next year. (10 minutes)' If it is likely that attendees are not experts (eg, don't know what a Balanced Score Card is), include a background reference so they can read up on it.

Keep agendas short; a meeting can't cover too many subjects effectively. And ruthlessly omit 'any other business'. This can cause howls of protest. It isn't always possible to know all topics in advance. Fine – so have an opportunity at the start of the meeting to add agenda items. If this makes the agenda too long, drop or postpone something else. Stick to the timings unless the meeting negotiates extra time for a subject, in which case be prepared to push something else out.

Feedback Agendas can be unnecessarily bureaucratic. By sticking to this checklist you can transform agendas without going over the top.

Outcome Good agendas make for shorter, better focused meetings that actually get something done.

Variations It is easiest to apply agenda management to your own meetings, but if someone else's meeting doesn't have a clear agenda, try to establish one at the start. All you need is a whiteboard or a sheet of paper on the table with the key headings written on it.

Managing yourself	✪✪
Managing other people	✪✪✪✪
Managing externals	✪
Business impact	✪✪✪✪
Social impact	✪✪
Fun	✪✪

4.25 | *Tasks, tasks*

Preparation None.
Running time Five minutes.
Resources Notebook.
Timescale Daily/weekly.

In *Chunking* (4.13) we see how focal activities are broken down into tasks. One section of your notebook should be a task list. This is a clear list of things to do. Each task should have a short description and a completion date. It is useful but not essential to link each task to a focal activity – certainly many tasks will be derived from them. Once a week it is sensible to check the focal activities and your task list to make sure there aren't new items to add.

Sometimes tasks are sensibly split up. For instance, one task in my focal activity of becoming a best-selling author might be writing this book. But writing a book is a lengthy task, so it can be broken down into components like writing the surrounding chapters, writing the exercises, checking the proofs and so on. Don't take tasks to too high a level of detail – it would be overkill to have a separate task for each of the exercises in this book – but ideally tasks should take no more than a week. I can break down writing the exercises into chunks, saying '10 completed by 10th November', or whatever.

Feedback The task list is driven by other sources, too, like meeting action points. Don't waste time by turning the task list into a project management exercise, marking the percentage completed each day.

Outcome The task list is an excellent overview. It is an essential tool in managing your work, and should also contain social activities to make sure they get a fair balance.

Variations The term 'notebook' is used loosely. It could be a conventional notebook, a ring binder, a time management system, an electronic personal organizer or a PIM. Electronic versions are particularly handy, as they can have alarms against key dates to make sure a task doesn't get forgotten. But the important thing is that your notebook suits you.

Managing yourself	✪✪✪✪
Managing other people	✪✪
Managing externals	✪✪
Business impact	✪✪✪✪
Social impact	✪✪✪✪
Fun	✪✪

4.26 | *Pareto*

Preparation None.
Running time Five minutes.
Resources None.
Timescale One-off.

When I first heard of this technique it was given the grand title Pareto Analysis – now it's more often called the 80:20 rule. A 19th century Italian economist called Vilfredo Pareto discovered that 80 per cent of the wealth was owned by 20 per cent of the people. Since then, this 80:20 rule has been found to apply in many circumstances.

The importance to time management is recognizing that you can often achieve 80 per cent completion with 20 per cent of the effort. The final polishing takes a huge 80 per cent. Sometimes that remainder is vital. You don't want a nuclear power plant that's 80 per cent safe. However, for most tasks (could it be 80 per cent of them?), 80 per cent success is fine. The Pareto rule explains one of the reasons PCs can be such time wasters. As we see in *PC plod* (4.53), it's tempting to use all those exciting features of your word processor to continue to refine the appearance of your letter (or form, or spreadsheet, or whatever) – with violently diminishing returns. When you are setting goals and milestones, wherever possible use an 80:20 target.

Feedback For some of us, Pareto is absolutely natural. We are happy with approximate solutions that do the job. For others it is a real wrench – a 'botched job'. This technique is not an excuse for sloppiness, but a plea for accepting a very good result rather than striving for perfection. Would this preclude the great works of art, the great theories of science ever being developed? Maybe, but lots of great thinkers and artists work very quickly – greatness isn't always about nit-picking.

Outcome The potential for freeing up time is enormous. If you moved everything from perfectionism to Pareto you would free up 80 per cent of your time. This isn't going to happen, but there is still a huge potential.

Variations Pareto could be one of your principles, see *Principles* (4.56).

Managing yourself	✪✪✪✪
Managing other people	✪✪✪
Managing externals	✪✪✪
Business impact	✪✪✪✪
Social impact	✪✪✪✪
Fun	✪✪

4.27 | *Garbage in, garbage out*

Preparation None.
Running time Variable.
Resources Meeting; notebook.
Timescale Ongoing.

Meetings are only as good as the output they generate. The purpose of this exercise is to maximize the valuable output of your next meeting, and to minimize the time-wasting output. Firstly, dispose of formal minutes. There is nothing more tedious to read. If you are required to keep a record for legal reasons, explore the practicalities of using audio tape. If even that is not possible, there is still no need to waste time and resources by sending out copies of minutes – just take them and file them.

In place of the formal minutes, generate action notes. These should state concisely what is to be done under whose charge by when. It may also say who is responsible for monitoring the action. It should be an exceptional meeting that generates more than one side of paper as action notes.

If your meeting is one of a series, there should be a running agenda item to feed back on the last action plan. This is not the same as a 'minutes of the last meeting' agenda item, which is all about nit-picking the minutes. The point is to establish what action has actually taken place and what remains to be done.

Feedback You might not have minutes – don't think this means you can get away without action notes – that's a recipe for meetings that go nowhere.

Outcome This approach cuts down on the time spent generating, reading and filing minutes, and reduces the danger of having meetings that result in no clear actions. If your action notes are blank for two meetings in a row, perhaps it's time to shut down that meeting.

Variations Action notes can be personalized (ie, just those actions you are responsible for) or for everyone. Usually it is worth giving them to everyone, as it acts as something of a spur to ensure that things get done.

Managing yourself	❂❂❂
Managing other people	❂❂❂❂
Managing externals	❂❂
Business impact	❂❂❂❂
Social impact	❂❂
Fun	❂

4.28 | *A little chat*

Preparation None.
Running time Five minutes.
Resources None.
Timescale One-off.

Some books on time management are deeply negative about social interaction. They teach you how to put people off, stopping them from distracting you. They help you to keep your conversations focused. There are some of these techniques in *Instant Time Management*. Yet the fact remains that social interaction is probably at the core of your life. Does that seem extreme? Think about your own circumstances. Despite the importance of social interaction, it probably won't be a focal activity, see *Focus* (4.8), and there's little point making it one. It's too woolly a concept. Yet you need to remember its importance.

Imagine this. You are at home and want to get everything tidy for the weekend. Then one of your best friends comes round and is really chatty. Half of you wants to talk, half wants to get rid of him/her. Challenge yourself. Think, what do I want to get things tidy for? So I can have a good social life, perhaps? So why ignore it? Unless you are a natural hermit, you actually want to be with people. You want to talk. It isn't an interruption, it's what's life is all about. You might make this a basis for one of your personal principles – see *Principles* (4.56).

Feedback   Of course it's important to stop the office bore from talking about his string collection for half an hour in the middle of the budget review. But there are plenty of social interactions – perhaps seeing your children in their nativity play, or having lunch with a friend – that are the whole point of your effort. Marginalizing them isn't the answer.

Outcome   It doesn't do any harm to get philosophical now and again. This exercise helps you to remember what the point of much of your activity really is.

Variations   You can repeat this exercise with more focused targets, for example, your children, your spouse, your close friends, etc.

Managing yourself	✪✪✪✪
Managing other people	✪✪✪
Managing externals	✪
Business impact	✪✪✪
Social impact	✪✪✪✪
Fun	✪✪✪

4.29 | *Penalizing pen pushing*

Preparation None.
Running time 10 minutes.
Resources None.
Timescale Annual.

This is an infrequent (once a year should be enough), but valuable exercise. Spend a few minutes thinking about the non-productive work you do. Filling in forms, administration, etc. Jot down a list of the main activities. Highlight those which happen very frequently or take a long time.

Now take the highlighted items. For each one consider three options. First, could you stop doing it all together? Would the world fall apart if you no longer filled in leave forms, but simply dropped your boss an e-mail? Would your business fail if you bought a packet of paperclips next time you are at the supermarket, rather than requisitioning them by filling in three forms in triplicate then waiting six weeks? Note which you can stop altogether. Next look at items you can get someone else to do. If you do have to have leave forms, can your staff process them themselves? Do you really need to be involved in paperclip purchase? Finally, if you must be involved, can you make your involvement less frequent, or do less? Could you authorize leave with a single signature, once a year? Could you buy paperclips by ticking a box on an on-line form?

Feedback   Don't spend too long on this exercise. When you've got the principle culprits sorted, stop – there's no point proceeding to the nth degree. Similarly, don't do it too frequently – bureaucracy is high in inertia, so it tends not to change too quickly.

Outcome   Time recovered from bureaucracy is win–win time. You get less bored, and the company gains time when you are doing something more productive. It's satisfying, too.

Variations   If you are very senior in your company, you can openly remove the bureaucracy. If you are junior and don't want to rock the boat, it may be more politic to get on with things quietly without making too much of a fuss about it.

Managing yourself	✪✪✪
Managing other people	✪✪✪✪
Managing externals	✪✪✪✪
Business impact	✪✪✪✪
Social impact	✪✪
Fun	✪✪✪

4.30 | **Letting go**

Preparation None.
Running time 10 minutes.
Resources None.
Timescale Monthly.

A big problem of time management is trying to do everything yourself. Almost everyone has some opportunity for delegation, yet many of us are reluctant to do it. Mostly it's a matter of trust. Will the other person get the job done? If they do it well, will they show us up? They can't win. You won't pick up effective delegation from a single exercise, but this technique will start you in the right direction. About once a month, think about what you actually do. How well do your actions fit with what you ought to be doing and what you do best? Your focal activities – *Focus* (4.8) – and talent list – *Talent spotting* (4.1) – will help. Highlight anything that deviates significantly, especially if it is time-consuming.

Now spend a couple of minutes thinking of potential delegates. Obvious candidates are your reports, your peers and your boss. There may be specific functions within your organization that could take on a job. Also think of external agencies, contractors and consultants. We live in an age of extended business structures – don't be parochial. Finally, aim to delegate at least one task or activity. You may manage several, but make sure something is given away.

Feedback A contract helps overcome difficulties with trust. This may just be desired outcomes and completion dates, but with more complex tasks or unknown delegates, it is sensible to include milestones. Many people find delegation a problem – see *Delegation difficulties* (4.51) for more help.

Outcome Provided you aren't giving responsibility without authority, you have a clear contract and you keep your hands off, delegation will free up plenty of time. If you prove good at it, you will also be considered a good manager and this will increase the respect of your staff.

Variations Delegation sideways and upwards has to be handled carefully if you aren't to be regarded as work-shy. It requires the positive agreement of those involved.

Managing yourself	✪✪✪✪
Managing other people	✪✪✪✪
Managing externals	✪✪✪
Business impact	✪✪✪✪
Social impact	✪✪✪
Fun	✪✪

4.31 | *Paper mountains*

Preparation None.
Running time Five minutes.
Resources Incoming documents.
Timescale Daily.

We all receive plenty of reading matter – letters, memos, magazines and so on. Like e-mails – see *The e-mail of the species* (4.9) – paper needs chunking. Don't read each item as it hits your desk, but pull them together at sensible intervals – perhaps once or twice a day – to fit your working pattern.

Take a couple of minutes over a first pass. Sort paper into three types. Junk, items requiring action and items requiring reading. Practise making this decision within a few seconds. Check the heading and the first paragraph – you ought to have made a decision by then. Commercial junk is probably best trashed, but reports and other internal documents are different. Write in large, red letters at the top (even better, get a stamp – it's very satisfying) 'Returned unread' and send it back. This is particularly valuable in a culture where you may be criticized for not taking action – here you have taken a very clear action.

Feedback   You may get people contacting you who assume you have read a document. You can try: honesty ('It didn't look relevant so I didn't read it' or 'I don't know'), distraction ('Remind me what it was about') or deception ('Yes?') Each is valid – see which suits you best.

Outcome   The principal aim is to avoid wasting time, but there are secondary benefits. By putting reading matter like magazines into a separate pile, you can chunk them up sensibly. And sending back items marked 'unread' may make the sender consider stopping the production of the offending article. Bear in mind, though the comments about self-preservation in Chapter 1 (see page 7).

Variations   Don't be tempted to split reading matter into categories – that's the level of detail where time management takes more time than it saves. However, you might find it useful to divide action items into 'today', 'this week' and 'this month'.

Managing yourself	✪✪
Managing other people	✪✪✪
Managing externals	✪✪✪✪
Business impact	✪✪✪✪
Social impact	✪✪
Fun	✪✪

4.32 | *Cherry picking*

Preparation None.
Running time Five minutes.
Resources None.
Timescale One-off.

A criticism of consultants is that they are always cherry picking, finding easy hits with a quick return so they look good. Cherry picking is something we all indulge in. Given a list of tasks, which do you choose to do first? The natural inclination is to do the things we enjoy and are comfortable with, and the tasks which are quick to finish with instant gratification. This can mean that important or time-dependent tasks get put off until it's too late.

Like many people, I don't like ringing up someone cold. Yet this is sometimes required for an interview. My natural tendency is to put off this call until the last possible moment. The trouble is, it can often take a week or two to get through. So leaving the calls to the day before the deadline can be a recipe for disaster. When it comes to choosing tasks to do first, always have the two essential criteria in mind. Is this task central to a focal activity, see *Focus* (4.8), and is it time critical?

Feedback While it is essential to use the two criteria mentioned above, it is also a good thing to have a steady flow of quick hits. They have two benefits – they boost your self-esteem and you are seen to be someone who delivers. As long as quick hits don't take up a high proportion of your time, they're beneficial.

Outcome Another exercise, *Priorities* (4.16), helps to choose the right tasks. This is more about avoiding the dangers of prevarication. Try writing 'No cherry picking' at the top of your task list.

Variations If you use an electronic task list with a prioritization feature you could set values of 1 for time critical and focal, 2 for time critical or focal and 3 for quick hits – but if this takes too long, don't bother – monitor cherry picking by eye.

Managing yourself	✪✪✪✪
Managing other people	✪
Managing externals	✪✪
Business impact	✪✪✪✪
Social impact	✪✪
Fun	✪✪

4.33 | *How wide is your door?*

Preparation None.
Running time Five minutes.
Resources None.
Timescale One-off.

Having an 'open door' policy has been a popular management technique for quite a while. In fact, many modern offices don't even have doors. But a policy like this is not really about furniture, it's about an attitude or frame of mind.

Spend a minute thinking about your own policy on accessibility. Do you have an ever-open door? Can anyone approach you? Or is your door welded solidly closed? Does someone need an appointment just to get sight of your PA? Where would you put yourself on the spectrum between open and closed?

If you haven't actually completed the previous step, go back and do it. Now.

There's no doubt that a closed door policy is a disaster. The message is that you don't care, the practicality is that you can't be brought into processes and decisions, so things take place despite you and you will become marginalized. Unfortunately, a totally open door, while better, isn't much better, because it is too easy to get swamped.

Feedback   The ideal is that you are readily accessible, but not necessarily all the time. This doesn't sound easy, but is quite practical, provided you work at it. It isn't an objective that can be achieved overnight as it will involve education of others, but it is entirely practical.

Outcome   This exercise isn't designed to control your accessibility. Many of the other exercises in this book will look at this from the direct physical control of *The red hat* (4.38) to controls on remote accessibility like the telephone and e-mail. For the moment it is enough to get a reasonable idea of your current status.

Variations   Ask some of your stakeholders – staff, customers, peers, bosses about your accessibility: see what they think. Think also about the effect on your time your current policy has. Is your level of accessibility using up a high percentage of your time?

Managing yourself	✪✪✪✪
Managing other people	✪✪✪✪
Managing externals	✪✪✪✪
Business impact	✪✪✪✪
Social impact	✪✪
Fun	✪✪

4.34 | *Failure rate*

Preparation None.
Running time 10 minutes.
Resources None.
Timescale Annual.

When things go wrong, your plans go out of the window and you switch into crisis mode. Occasionally this is inevitable. However, too often we find ourselves accepting regular failure as a necessary part of life, because we don't do anything to prevent it.

Think back over the last year. Note down things that went wrong – big things and small things. Look for contributory factors that are shared by several failures. Quite often we know about a problem, but are so busy getting on with the job that we don't take the time to fix it. A popular time management metaphor is sharpening the saw – too many of us are so busy cutting that we don't take time to sharpen the saw and so everything takes longer than it needs to. Where you have identified a common thread, set up a task (or an activity if it is significant enough) to do something about it.

Feedback The nature of these common threads is quite varied. For instance, you may find that a lot of problems resulted from a breakdown in communications. Perhaps your own communication skills need an overhaul. It might be worth setting up a whole activity to deal with this. Alternatively, it could be something as simple as wasting lots of time because you can never get through to the Internet to pick up your e-mail, so you need a task to change the e-mail provider.

Outcome Failure is inevitable and good as long as we learn from it. This exercise is designed to weed out repeated, tolerated failure. The sort where we don't learn, and waste much time re-inventing the wheel.

Variations You may find this effective more than once a year. If you have trouble remembering what went wrong (the memory is good at suppressing failure), keep a failure log. It needn't take much time and can result in massive improvements if you catch a big repetitive problem.

Managing yourself	✪✪✪✪
Managing other people	✪✪✪
Managing externals	✪✪✪
Business impact	✪✪✪✪
Social impact	✪✪✪✪
Fun	✪✪

4.35 | *A file in a cake*

Preparation None.
Running time 15 minutes.
Resources None.
Timescale One-off.

This one's about filing – but don't stop reading now, it won't be too painful. The essential tool is a good set of trays. These can be stacked trays, drawers, piles on the floor (bear in mind the warning in Chapter 1 about appearances – see page 7) – whatever suits you. The first part of this exercise is to set them up. Label a set of trays (if you haven't any, use an alternative and change later if required). Most people need in, out, read, today, this week, file. You may have other requirements. I have expenses and tax, because I operate a small business.

Now you need two disciplines. The first is to use the trays properly. When papers arrive, they go straight into in. When you deal with paper – see *Paper Mountains* (4.31) – make sure items go into one of the trays (or the bin). Don't let anything stay in the in tray, or go into limbo. Oh, and check daily if anything should move from this week to today. The second discipline is the filing. It should be regular, but not too often – perhaps weekly. As you pass through your file tray, attempt to throw things away – many lawsuits have proved the dangers of hanging on to paper – if you must file it, make sure there's an appropriate folder. If not, set one up. If you can't be bothered to set up a folder, bin it.

Feedback These trays sound a bureaucrat's dream. They're not; you are performing triage. By forcing everything into a tray, it's out of the way, leaving you to get on with real work.

Outcome This exercise is about freedom from the pressure of a pile of incoming items. It structures your input, making it easier to handle.

Variations If your filing needs are small, handle it directly, rather than having a filing tray.

Managing yourself	✪✪✪✪
Managing other people	✪✪
Managing externals	✪✪✪✪
Business impact	✪✪✪✪
Social impact	✪✪
Fun	✪

4.36 | *Little treats*

Preparation None.
Running time Five minutes.
Resources Notebook.
Timescale Ongoing.

Sometimes it makes good time management sense to stop working. No one can do brain work for hours on end and maintain efficiency – 90 minutes is about the limit before serious degradation sets in. A first step can be a change of air and position. Get up, perhaps go outside for a couple of minutes – air conditioning and heating sap your energy. Get yourself a cup of coffee or look at a magazine.

If you are engaged in an all-day task you will need more diverting breaks. Keep a list of bite-sized mini-projects in your notebook. These should take up little time, and be diverting, but not urgent. To be effective, you should be able to complete something in a few minutes. When you are working on a lengthy, high-pressure project, divert into a treat for a few minutes every couple of hours.

Feedback It can be difficult to do this. Under pressure, you want to spend every minute on the subject at hand. But this will lead to inefficient use of your time as you lose concentration. Force yourself to take a few minutes out. Of course, there will be circumstances when you are on a roll, everything is flowing and you really don't need a break. Don't follow this approach slavishly, but do bring it in when needed.

Outcome Five minutes diversion will be repaid with a much greater equivalent increase in effectiveness. An essential ingredient is that the treat tasks are things that you enjoy doing (however menial), and that there is a clear completion in a few minutes. There is something wonderful about completion.

Variations Turn this exercise upside down to capture treats when they aren't appropriate. If you find yourself thinking 'Oh, I wish I could just do X' and you know it is prevarication, jot it down in on your treats list, knowing that you will do it in due time.

Managing yourself	✪✪✪✪
Managing other people	✪
Managing externals	✪
Business impact	✪✪✪✪
Social impact	✪✪✪✪
Fun	✪✪✪✪

4.37 | *Scheduling admin*

Preparation *A file in a cake* (4.35).
Running time Five minutes.
Resources None.
Timescale Daily/weekly.

Meet yourself half way (4.17) mentions the need to schedule administrative tasks. This takes more attention than you might think. Admin needs a firm hand to keep it under control.

Before doing this exercise, make sure you have completed *A file in a cake* (4.35). Having done so, you should have a neat system of trays. But what to do with them? Each day needs slots in your diary for dealing with paper, phone calls and e-mails. Remember also to have some slack time for reading. You can schedule this (I like lunch time), or use it to distract yourself when you are losing impetus on a piece of work – but if you take the latter approach, make sure it doesn't disappear.

When everything is neatly sorted into trays, though, your day isn't over (unless you are a filing clerk). At the start or end of each week, get a rough plan for the week ahead. Check your task list, see *Tasks, tasks* (4.25). Look through anything already in the this week tray. Rough out appropriate slots in your diary. Each day, perhaps after your first quick pass through the paper and e-mails, firm up the day's plan, taking account of the Today tray and your task list. The aim should be to have disposed of appropriate items by the end of the day. You won't always succeed – planning is inherently guesswork – but you've got something to aim for.

Feedback   This sounds more complicated than it is; try it.

Outcome   A routine like this makes time management possible. Without it, admin takes over or doesn't get done and you have regular crises.

Variations   Exactly how you arrange this is down to your personal approach. Remember the different times of day at which you perform different tasks best, *Hot spots* (4.7).

Managing yourself	✪✪✪✪
Managing other people	✪✪
Managing externals	✪✪✪✪
Business impact	✪✪✪✪
Social impact	✪✪
Fun	✪

4.38 | *The red hat*

Preparation Obtain a red baseball cap.
Running time Two minutes.
Resources No special requirements.
Timescale Ongoing.

Unnecessary interruptions are a common problem when attempting to manage your time better. You have spent half an hour getting an idea together in your head, when someone asks if you saw *The X-files* on TV the other night, or wants the telephone number of a print company. Any other time, you'd be happy to talk, but right now you need to concentrate.

The technique is simple. Get hold of a red baseball cap. Let it be widely known that when you are wearing the cap, you are not available for comment. Anything less than emergencies should wait. Don't overuse this technique. You shouldn't normally have the cap on for more than half a day, or it becomes just another barrier to communication.

Feedback It will take a while for the message to sink in. Initially you will still get interruptions – respond politely, but point out why you've got the hat on. The word will quickly get round.

Outcome If you handle interruptions when you've got the cap on very positively, you'll find red hats spring up all over; do it badly and you'll lose a lot of friends. This technique is particularly valuable in open plan offices, where the temptation to call across is very strong. A side effect of this approach can be to help to concentrate your mind on a task – the act of putting on the cap keeps your own attention focused.

Variations It needn't be a baseball cap. Try a flag on your desk or a bright red jacket. Whatever you use must be clearly visible from a distance, as the requirement is to stop an interruption from ever starting. It's too late when they're standing by your desk. Some companies allow the use of personal stereos – provided the headphones are obvious (put red ends on them) – these too can act as a warning that you do not want to be disturbed.

Managing yourself	✪✪
Managing other people	✪✪✪✪
Managing externals	✪
Business impact	✪✪✪✪
Social impact	✪✪
Fun	✪✪

4.39 | *We have contact*

Preparation None.
Running time 10 minutes.
Resources Notebook.
Timescale Monthly.

An effective contact list is a powerful tool in your business. Although peripheral to time management, it is worth including here because it intertwines with so many of the key elements of time management. The three keys to survival and thriving in the modern business world are creativity, communication and knowledge. Linking these is your network of contacts, and keeping track of them, having ready access to their phone and fax numbers – real-world and electronic addresses – is a basic requirement.

When you are processing paper or e-mails or calls, be prepared to update your contact list, because you don't want to sort through 500 business cards and letterheads to find a telephone number. On a regular basis, perhaps monthly, flick through your contacts book. Weed out obvious dead wood. Try to generate a few tasks – there are bound to be some contacts that you should have been in touch with to further one of your focal activities.

Feedback   As always, balance is sensible. Keep essential information. Add additional information, provided you may make use of it. If it's easy to capture you might as well. Note that in the UK you can hold a personal address book on a computer without registering with the Data Protection Registrar, but a shared address book or company resource will need registration.

Outcome   Keeping your network fresh is an essential. Your contacts list is a positive driver for action.

Variations   The term 'notebook' is used loosely. I've seen it work well as a conventional notebook, a ring binder, a time management system, an electronic personal organizer or a PIM. Electronic versions are particularly handy, as addresses can be fed straight into word processors or e-mail packages. With the right technology you can also initiate phone calls and send faxes. But the important thing is that your notebook suits you.

Managing yourself	❍❍❍
Managing other people	❍❍❍❍
Managing externals	❍❍
Business impact	❍❍❍❍
Social impact	❍❍❍❍
Fun	❍❍

4.40 | *Floor plan*

Preparation None.
Running time Five minutes.
Resources Paper.
Timescale One-off.

Take a look at the layout of your work area, whether it's an office or a chunk of open plan space. Draw it roughly on a piece of paper, using separate slips of paper to represent moveable objects like a desk or partitions. Spend a couple of minutes trying out alternative layouts and the advantages or disadvantages these make. Look particularly at what is near your desk. Also give some thought to the way your desk is oriented. Does it face the door/access way? How is it positioned with respect to any windows?

Consider making a change to your space. Look for opportunities to make your use of the space more efficient and to maximize your time management.

Feedback Exactly how you arrange things is going to depend on you, what you do and your space. If you make frequent use of books, is there any way of getting the bookcase closer to your desk? If the filing cabinet is something you rarely use, why has it such a prominent spot? Orientation of your desk is more subtle. Turning your back on the door will reduce the number of drop-in callers you get, but may make you feel anxious. If you use a computer screen you will want to be oriented to avoid glare from the window. At the same time, you might want a position where you can look out of the window when you want to, but ensure it doesn't form an active distraction (blinds can help).

Outcome We rarely give as much thought to arranging our workspace as we do to our home environment, yet we typically spend many hours a week in it. A few minutes thought could really reap rewards.

Variations If you have an appropriate graphics package on your PC you can use that to draw your plan, but don't be tempted to spend too long over it.

Managing yourself	✪✪✪
Managing other people	✪✪
Managing externals	✪✪✪✪
Business impact	✪✪✪✪
Social impact	✪
Fun	✪✪✪

4.41 | *How long?*

Preparation None.
Running time Five minutes.
Resources Diary.
Timescale One-off.

The purpose of this activity is to set a target for dividing your time between work and personal activities. Using your diary if it's helpful, get an idea how many hours in a week you spend on work activities (if you've already done the activity *Where'd it go?* (4.6), you should have your information already). Include any work you take home. Taking out sleeping time, check what that leaves for personal activities (there are 168 hours in a week, so with a seven hour sleep, you have around 115 to 120 usable hours a week).

Is that balance what you'd really like? Be honest – don't try to match the expectations of your company or your family, what would you really like to do? Look at the difference on a daily basis. How many hours a day would you like to move from work to personal, or personal to work? Perhaps you've got the balance just right, in which case there is no more to do. More often than not, you haven't.

Consider making it one of your focal activities to move this balance in your preferred direction.

Feedback Few people can make changes like this overnight, but it doesn't make the change any less desirable or possible. Changing might mean changing the way you work – more and more people are opting for flexible careers with a portfolio of tasks; more and more companies use consultants and contractors – or it may simply mean using different values when you decide when to go home. But remember, you've only got one attempt to get your life right: don't waste it.

Outcome This activity doesn't have an immediate effect, but sets an agenda item. It is, however, important.

Variations Work and personal is the most obvious split, but you might consider different splits like paying/non-paying work, work at different levels of pay, working from home versus commuting and so on.

Managing yourself	❍❍❍❍
Managing other people	❍❍
Managing externals	❍❍
Business impact	❍❍❍❍
Social impact	❍❍❍❍
Fun	❍❍

4.42 | *Crowd control*

Preparation Must be performed in advance.
Running time Two minutes.
Resources Meeting; notebook.
Timescale Ongoing.

In *Agenda bender* (4.24) we looked at the meeting agenda – equally important is the invitee list. Treat this as an exercise for the next meeting you organize and the next meeting you attend. All too often meetings consist of the wrong people, and quite frequently there are too many bodies present.

If you are arranging a meeting, consider who needs to be present. Who is a key stakeholder? Who has necessary expertise? Use these considerations to build an initial list. For a meeting that is intended to decide something (as opposed to an information dissemination meeting), it is desirable to keep numbers in single figures – between two and eight is ideal. Be aware that ongoing meetings almost always grow. People want to get involved, to find out what is going on, to make sure that they are represented or to enhance personal power. Be firm with your meetings – take someone off if another person is added.

If you attend a meeting, ask yourself 'why?' Could someone else go instead? Does anyone from your area need to go at all? Are there better ways to get the input or information you need from the meeting? Need there be a meeting at all?

Feedback   Start by questioning the existence of a meeting. If it has to exist, give serious thought to who should attend, and why you attend any meetings you go to.

Outcome   Less people at less meetings means more individual time available for productive work, and more effective meetings that don't get bogged down in the interplay of so many people.

Variations   Consider replacing meetings with electronic discussion groups. Beware the argument that says such an approach is bad, as it degrades face-to-face contact. You can still have plenty of face-to-face contact, but it needn't take up anywhere near so much time, and can be more socially beneficial.

Managing yourself	✪✪
Managing other people	✪✪✪✪
Managing externals	✪
Business impact	✪✪✪✪
Social impact	✪✪
Fun	✪✪

4.43 | *Rampant reading*

Preparation None.
Running time 10 minutes.
Resources None.
Timescale One-off.

If you have too much reading matter, it is important to cut down your input – see *Paper mountains* (4.31). But you may still need to read a lot. Try a couple of techniques to increase your speed.

These techniques use a visual guide. This is nothing new. You used one when you first began to read – your finger. In fact, the guide can still be your finger, or the blunt end of a pen or pencil – any pointer you are comfortable holding while reading. There's one big difference, though. Instead of pointing at each word in turn, run the guide smoothly along under the text. Start at your habitual reading speed, then notch up the speed. You will find a marked increase in reading rate over a short period of practice.

When you are comfortable with the guide, try a different method. Instead of moving the guide along the text, move it down the centre of the page. It is entirely possible to pick up the meaning of whole lines of text by interpolation. You can't read every word this way, but it is a highly efficient way of skimming. The technique takes a little longer to get the hang of, but is well worth acquiring.

Feedback Using a visual guide might make you feel uncomfortable. After all, you did this at junior school. There, though, the finger followed the speed with which you could recognize words. Now the guide leads your eyes. However, because of infantile associations, you may find a pencil end less embarrassing than a finger.

Outcome These complementary techniques will increase your speed of detailed reading and your skimming speed. The simple guide alone has been shown to increase reading speeds by between 50 and 100 per cent.

Variations There are various other speed reading techniques, some involving considerable training, but the two mentioned above have the advantage of requiring little effort for considerable advantage.

Managing yourself	✪✪✪✪
Managing other people	✪✪
Managing externals	✪✪✪✪
Business impact	✪✪✪✪
Social impact	✪✪✪
Fun	✪✪

4.44 | *We don't deliver*

Preparation None.
Running time Five minutes.
Resources None.
Timescale One-off.

A lot of people don't deliver on time. They say they will do something by a date. They may even sign a piece of paper to this effect. Then they seem surprised when they don't deliver – or even worse, they don't seem to care. If you regularly fail to deliver on time, your time management has failed. What's more, it will continue to fail because uncompleted tasks will impact the next things you planned to do.

If you believe delivering, and being seen to deliver, is important, you need to make realistic estimates. We shorten estimates to be competitive and to please – but it's better to estimate 10 per cent over and come in on time. Even if your estimates are good, things will go wrong. That's where you can make a big difference. By putting 150 per cent effort into recovering from an overrun, and keeping your stakeholders aware of what is going on, you will gain recognition and retain control of your time. It will mean the occasional change of priorities at late notice, but it will be worth it. Check the timings of your current priority tasks. Are they realistic? Should you change anything? How about the timing of recent failures and successes?

Feedback This technique is not about living from crisis to crisis. If you are always pulling out the stops to fix problems, you've got the estimating wrong.

Outcome Surprising though it may seem in a consumer-driven society, delivering the goods on time is a rarity. Succeed and you will not only have good time management, you shouldn't go short of a job either.

Variations How you manage your estimates is outside the remit of this book, but bear in mind that forecasting is guesswork. Don't estimate something you know approximately to three decimal places. Planning works better with ballpark figures and a few milestones than grinding detail, and such plans are much easier to change at a moment's notice, too.

Managing yourself	✪✪✪✪
Managing other people	✪✪
Managing externals	✪✪
Business impact	✪✪✪✪
Social impact	✪✪✪
Fun	✪✪

4.45 | *The secretary's secret*

Preparation None.
Running time 10 minutes.
Resources A secretary/PA.
Timescale One-off.

If you haven't got a secretary, ignore this one. If you have one, spend a few minutes jotting down what your secretary does. Try to group the activities into broad categories like communications and diary management. Once this is done, you can examine possible changes.

I have seen time management books suggesting that a secretary's prime role is as a barrier. A defence against everyone who is determined to waste your time. This is a poor use of a secretary. You ought to be answering your own e-mail (although your secretary may well filter it first), and doing it directly onto the screen. You ought, at least part of the time, to be answering your own telephone, see *Telephone tag* (4.23); and you ought to do your own typing. There is no excuse these days for anyone to have poor keyboard skills, and retyping is a waste of time and effort. Some conventional tasks remain. Diary management makes sense, provided your secretary knows to leave the gaps you need, see *Meet yourself half way* (4.17). Filtering and preprocessing paper is a boon. But the modern secretary ought to be a PA. Someone you can assign a task to and get it done with your own approach and authority.

Feedback Many secretaries remain fanatical guardians cum typists. Neither role is suited to modern business. Although some are susceptible to retraining, many aren't. It makes for a difficult decision.

Outcome The transformed secretary is a marvel of time management, because he/she extends the time in a day – now you have an alter ego to take on some of your tasks.

Variations It is possible to have a number of these PAs, representing you in different ways. It is necessary to keep an eye out for the power-lover who wants your authority without responsibility, but with careful selection you can extend your time across four or five people.

Managing yourself	✪✪✪
Managing other people	✪✪✪✪
Managing externals	✪✪✪
Business impact	✪✪✪✪
Social impact	✪✪
Fun	✪✪

4.46 | *Going walkabout*

Preparation None.
Running time 10 minutes.
Resources Feet.
Timescale Daily.

Management by walking about (MBWA) is an old chestnut that is as valuable today as it always has been. In fact, the increasing tendency to have open plan offices makes it even more attractive.

The idea is that at least once a day you make a tour of the area you work in. This isn't checking-up, but making yourself plainly available. It is difficult to get the hang of initially, as people should approach you if they want to, but not be interrupted if they don't. A handy prop to make this more natural is the coffee machine – make sure you use the communal coffee facilities at least once a day even if you have an overly efficient secretary, and make your route there and back leisurely.

Feedback   Expect this one to take a while to sink in. If you aren't already practising MBWA, people probably won't talk to you to begin with. But as it becomes a regular, expected thing, they will make use of it.

Outcome   This approach is beneficial as a general management technique, but also has time management implications. If you want to reduce the number of interruptions you get when concentrating on something, this conscious exposure of yourself at a time you control will relieve some of the pressure. People would rather talk to you in an informal setting than disturb you at your desk – this approach sanctions that process.

Variations   If you are lucky enough to work in an environment which has carefully thought out shared space – typically a large, under-glass area of boulevards and cafes in cooler climates – you can have a variant of this approach by making sure you take at least one coffee break a day at the expresso bar (or whatever). Ideally, this is a supplement to walking about in the work area, as it exposes you to a different set of people.

Managing yourself	●●
Managing other people	●●●●
Managing externals	●●●
Business impact	●●●●
Social impact	●●
Fun	●●●

4.47 | *Deflecting distraction*

Preparation None.
Running time Two minutes.
Resources None.
Timescale Ongoing.

However much you want to concentrate on what you are doing, there will be people who consider it their right to wander in and chat. In *The red hat* (4.38) we looked at signalling 'I don't want to be disturbed', but sometimes the person gets through. There are a number of techniques to deflect the distraction.

Some activities make you less likely to be disturbed. If you see a potential distraction on the way, you can start a phone conversation (real or imaginary), hunch over your keyboard or pad and start to write frantically, or grab someone and engage in an obviously personal conversation. Other mechanisms like taking your clothes off or blatantly picking your nose will work, but won't help your reputation.

You can remove yourself from the equation by leaving ('sorry, must rush, urgent meeting') and slip into the toilet or work somewhere other than your desk, see *Quiet corners* (4.15) and *Home sweet home* (4.48).

Feedback If the distracter doesn't take the hint, shorten the distraction by reducing your responsiveness (avoid eye contact, use single word or grunts as reply, look frequently at your watch). If this fails, resort to the polite explicit, 'Sorry, I'm going to have to cut this short now, I've got something to finish for the boss and I'm dead meat if I don't get started'.

Outcome Interruptions have a greater impact on your work than their length implies. Any significant task requires a fair amount of stacking up of thoughts before getting started – any interruption can totally shatter your house of cards. These techniques should be used sparingly, but will help to reduce painful interruptions.

Variations A useful approach if conversation can't be avoided is to take the politician's approach of turning everything round to what you want to say. Whatever they come to talk about, make sure you end up offloading work on them. They may soon take the hint.

Managing yourself	✪✪
Managing other people	✪✪✪✪
Managing externals	✪✪
Business impact	✪✪✪✪
Social impact	✪✪
Fun	✪✪

4.48 | *Home, sweet home*

Preparation None.
Running time 10 minutes.
Resources None.
Timescale One-off.

This is a planning exercise – you aren't going to change your working pattern in 10 minutes. Working in an office has big advantages, but it is also loaded with distractions. It can be very helpful to spend some time working from home, not taking work home outside office hours, but being at home in working time.

Spend a few minutes thinking about the benefits of home working. For most people this might be one to three days a week, not the whole time. Think of the advantages for you and for the company. They might include less distraction, less commuting time, better productivity, more comfort, more contact with the family. Then spend a couple of minutes thinking of the disadvantages. They might include unsuitable premises, your boss doesn't know what you are doing, more family distraction, harder to contact. Put this together as a balance sheet. If the outcome is strongly positive, make the move to home working a focal activity, see *Focus* (4.8).

Feedback Mainly due to a lack of trust, implementation of home working has been very slow. Unless your company supports it, your options are to change company, to become self-employed or to support any initiatives (volunteering for any pilot schemes). For the company to achieve maximum financial benefit, it may combine homeworking with hot-desking, where desks are not personally owned, reducing office space. This forces an orderly approach, but does have an administrative overhead.

Outcome This exercise should explore your valuation of home working. Depending on the outcome you may start pushing in this direction – those who have done so voluntarily usually feel it makes a huge difference to their personal productivity and time management.

Variations There are a variety of alternative schemes, like small local satellite offices, with a similar effect to home working, but usually with less time management benefit.

Managing yourself	⊙⊙⊙⊙
Managing other people	⊙⊙⊙⊙
Managing externals	⊙⊙⊙⊙
Business impact	⊙⊙⊙⊙
Social impact	⊙⊙⊙⊙
Fun	⊙⊙⊙

4.49 | *Be prepared*

Preparation None.
Running time 10 minutes.
Resources Staff.
Timescale One-off.

This exercise assumes you have staff reporting to you. Communication with your staff is vital – it's one of the most important parts of your job, but such communication can become obtrusive. Other techniques look at deflecting interruptions or channelling them – it's even better to train your staff to interrupt more efficiently.

Next time you have a team meeting, assign 10 minutes to this issue. Explain your problem and give them a couple of minutes to come up with possible ways of making their communication with you more effective. Take the best ideas and add in any of the following which aren't already there.

- Send low priority information by e-mail.
- Keep everything but high priority communication for an agreed time of day.
- Package your communication to get across any necessary information, then present the need for action or a decision.
- Have some recommendations, rather than expecting solutions there and then.
- Have a realistic idea of how long the interruption will take, and check it up front.
- Produce a mini-agenda for the discussion.

Feedback This has to be handled diplomatically. Everyone may know that your time is important and in short supply, but there's nothing to gain from rubbing their noses in it. Expect to issue gentle reminders to begin with – running in to say something is a habit and needs some breaking.

Outcome Anything you can do to encourage others to manage their interruptions for you is a superb piece of time management, because you are delegating the management task. Also the conscious effort of structuring their interruption will cause a fair number of low priority disruptions never to occur.

Variations This technique can be put across by edict rather than the quasi-democratic approach here, but it will have less impact.

Managing yourself	✪✪
Managing other people	✪✪✪✪
Managing externals	✪✪✪
Business impact	✪✪✪✪
Social impact	✪
Fun	✪✪

4.50 | *Nota bene*

Preparation None.
Running time Two minutes.
Resources Notebook.
Timescale Ongoing.

Notes are very valuable. Not only can you refer back to them, the very action of taking notes reinforces information in your memory. However, it is impossible to be definitive about a good note format. Many effective time managers keep changing their approach. Some find large hardback notebooks best. Everything is in chronological order. Old books are filed for retrieval. The great thing about this approach is that you don't need to do anything else. A ring binder approach, whether large format or a time management system, is more flexible, but you need a regular clear out to prevent your binder getting too fat. Journalists still swear by spiral bound pads.

I personally prefer a small pad (a police notebook or an electronic personal organizer) that can be kept with me at all times. That way, when the need to make a note strikes, it can be captured immediately. Supplement this with a large pad when you are somewhere that needs copious notes, for instance an information dissemination meeting – see *Notes with attitude* (4.70) for more on the structured note taking that is particularly effective here. Finally, take the effort to put notes that need to be searched on PC, whether as a word processor document or in a more structured form.

Feedback Try a range of options, but avoid scraps of paper that get lost. Sticky notes are great, but only as an attention grabber. If you need to remind yourself to do something tomorrow morning, they are great. But once there is a fringe of notes surrounding your PC screen, you have lost the battle. They are a distraction without being an alert. Sticky notes should be restricted to immediate action.

Outcome Notes are an essential extension and support for your memory. Sensible use pays off richly.

Variations The term 'notebook' is used loosely here. The important thing is that your notebook suits you.

Managing yourself	✪✪✪✪
Managing other people	✪
Managing externals	✪✪
Business impact	✪✪✪✪
Social impact	✪✪✪✪
Fun	✪✪

4.51 | *Delegation difficulties*

Preparation None.
Running time Five minutes.
Resources People to delegate to.
Timescale One-off.

Many of us find delegation difficult (note by the way, this exercise applies even if you don't have staff – you still delegate, whether by asking a peer to do something for you or paying a cleaner to tidy your house). In this short exercise we will start to address the problem.

Spend a couple of minutes writing down why you find delegation difficult. If you think you don't, write down why others might. Only then check the list below.

- You know you can do it better.
- It's your job to keep a tight rein.
- You are insecure.
- You aren't sure of your own role.
- The other people have enough to do.
- The job needs a recognized figure.

Each of these reasons – and any others you may have come up with – has a counter. Spend the remaining time thinking of specific counters to each reason.

Feedback Only you can really counter your own objections: this one goes beyond logic. Some answers will be as simple as 'so what?' This is a good response, for example to 'You know you can do it better' – as long as they can do a satisfactory job, so what? Others will require you to find something out or take a risk with people. Unless you can, you aren't going to gain their trust or their full input. In the end, if they aren't good enough to delegate to, why do you work with them?

Outcome Delegation is essential to effective time management – there are very few roles which you can truly undertake alone. In the end, delegation is only learnt by doing it. Take the risk and see what happens.

Variations Instead of coming at the problems of delegation by examining the arguments against it, list the advantages of delegation. Then use these as arguments for doing it.

Managing yourself	✪✪✪✪
Managing other people	✪✪✪✪
Managing externals	✪✪
Business impact	✪✪✪✪
Social impact	✪✪✪
Fun	✪✪

4.52 | *Reading up*

Preparation None.
Running time Five minutes.
Resources None.
Timescale One-off.

Reading is an important activity in almost all contexts, yet it is often given a low worth. To be seen sitting at your desk reading a book or a magazine (even a business book or magazine) is generally considered to be only one step above being asleep. Yet whether your intention is to be more effective at your job, to know more about a hobby or to expand your personal creativity, reading is essential.

Because of the disparity between actual value and perceived value, reading needs special treatment. Spend a couple of minutes going through your typical reading matter for a week. Consider non-fiction and fiction, books, magazines and newspapers. Now try to put together a picture of your ideal reading content. Set some realistic targets, like a novel a week, a business book a week, etc.

Finally allocate appropriate slots to reading. Because of the perceived low value, it will be necessary to make these in your less exposed time (unless you work in a particularly enlightened business) – but there should be no excuse for putting reading off. Reading can fit into a lower energy slot than some activities, see *Hot spots* (4.7), but don't choose a time when it will put you to sleep.

Feedback　The disparity is an odd one, which you may find it valuable to discuss with your boss. Why is it that we are quite prepared to send someone off on a course for days at a time, but don't like to see someone reading a business book for half an hour? In fact such a discussion may even result in legitimizing a business reading slot.

Outcome　If you can pull reading on to a par with administration in priorities you will be achieving more than most people, and ensuring that you gain a personal edge.

Variations　Look at different sources of reading material: libraries, bookshops, Internet bookshops, learning centres within the company.

Managing yourself	✪✪✪✪
Managing other people	✪✪
Managing externals	✪✪✪
Business impact	✪✪✪✪
Social impact	✪✪✪✪
Fun	✪✪✪

4.53 | *PC plod*

Preparation None.
Running time Five minutes.
Resources Personal computer.
Timescale One-off.

Many of us could no longer work without a personal computer. It is only when your PC breaks, or there's a power cut that you realize how dependent you have become. But the PC has time management dangers, which are worth assessing. Specifically, the PC can become an administrative distraction, and can over-stress perfection. The administrative distraction comes from the fact that it is easy to spend hours getting your PC arranged the way you want it. Such activity is not a bad short break – see *Little treats* (4.36), but it shouldn't be allowed to stray into prime time.

Perfection is a problem because it is usually possible to make a series of small improvements, which take lots of time but have relatively little value. A classic example would be production of reports in a modern word processor, where no end of time can be spent altering fonts and boxes and margins to get the right look. This is not advocating a return to typewritten documents – they now seem virtually unreadable. It is, however a plea to apply *Pareto* analysis (see 4.26), and make sure you get the 80 per cent of the look in 20 per cent of the time.

Feedback Some PC fiddling is 'saw sharpening' – spending a few minutes improving the tool that will result in a lot more savings. For instance, many people do not use templates in word processors, yet these can greatly increase productivity when producing standard documents.

Outcome Careful tuning of your PC use can change it from a time waster to a valuable tool.

Variations Learning how to use your PC software better will reduce time wasted. Don't assume, though, that this means lengthy training in specific software. The essentials are a good grasp of how to use Windows (or the equivalent), and practice at exploration: finding what is available quickly and effectively.

Managing yourself	⊙⊙⊙
Managing other people	⊙
Managing externals	⊙⊙⊙⊙
Business impact	⊙⊙⊙⊙
Social impact	⊙⊙⊙
Fun	⊙⊙

4.54 | *It's mine*

Preparation None.
Running time Five minutes.
Resources None.
Timescale One-off.

This exercise looks at a delegation problem that is particularly strong in the social arena. There are all sorts of tasks which tradition allocates to the householder. He or she is expected to do the decorating and minor repairs, and to keep the garden looking good. Similarly a car owner is expected to sort out minor problems, and so on. This emotional pressure, often associated with sexual stereotyping ('what sort of man can't put up a shelf/ change a spark plug?', 'what sort of woman can't cook a meal/iron?') is surprisingly strong. Spend a couple of minutes listing the typical chores in your social life – include the activities of everyone in your close family.

Now split them up into those you enjoy doing (don't ask me why, but I like going to the supermarket, for instance) or feel you get personal benefit from, and those you hate. Against each 'hate' put a high, medium or low cost mark. Use an average hourly rate for your pay as medium, anything significantly more as high, and significantly less as low. Consider paying someone to do any low cost tasks. There are a lot better uses of your time.

Feedback Delegating is different in the domestic environment. It's clearer that you are moving a scarce time resource from a chore to something you'd like to be doing, but the emotional pressures are stronger too. Make sure you do something specific with the time you freed up – that way you can really appreciate the benefit.

Outcome Shifting chunks of social time away from unwanted chores generates real benefit for your time management. And giving someone a job, too – can't be bad.

Variations Although this technique is specifically designed for social time management, it is applicable at work, too. An alternative approach is turning a chore into something you enjoy doing by having the right tools, training or motivation.

Managing yourself	✪✪✪✪
Managing other people	✪✪✪
Managing externals	✪✪
Business impact	✪✪✪
Social impact	✪✪✪✪
Fun	✪✪

4.55 | *TV turn-off*

Preparation None.
Running time Two minutes.
Resources TV.
Timescale Ongoing.

The television is probably the biggest waster of your social time. This isn't a criticism of TV – it is a simple fact. Few people list watching TV as a focal activity, see *Focus* (4.8), yet most of us spend five to 20 hours a week watching it – a fair percentage of the time that isn't allocated to work or sleep.

I am not advocating giving up the television set. However, if you do find that your time to build on your social activities is limited, consider a few simple actions. Limit yourself to a single programme a day – if necessary, use a video recorder to time shift everything else. Limit your viewing time most days, with one 'splurge' day when you can watch a whole film or feature-length programme.

If you find this difficult, give your viewing a rough ranking and drop some of the lowest rated programmes. Be honest about this ranking – it's only for you. Don't use the traditional 'cultured' view that puts news ahead of arts programmes ahead of documentaries, then the rest – if you like soap operas, they get the highest ranking.

Feedback We all have days when we are totally worn out and want to slump in front of the TV. There's nothing wrong with this at all, provided it is some days, rather than all days.

Outcome If time freed up from TV viewing is used well – making sure that it is concentrated on the social activities that you have decided are among your focal activities – it is a superb source of extra time.

Variations Some people find it helpful to record all the TV programmes they might watch, finding that in practice they don't watch nearly so many this way. This has limitations when it comes to live broadcasts, but can otherwise be very useful.

Managing yourself	❍❍❍
Managing other people	❍
Managing externals	❍❍❍❍
Business impact	❍❍
Social impact	❍❍❍❍
Fun	❍❍❍

4.56 | *Principles*

Preparation None.
Running time Five minutes.
Resources Notebook or sheet of paper.
Timescale One-off.

Time management systems can go mad with different levels of breakdown. You need a mission, objectives, goals, activities and tasks... and wonder why you never do anything but fill in bits of paper. This exercise seems worrying, because it generates yet another category, but it's a very different one. Some time management gurus recommend having a mission statement, but I find they make me nauseous. The first exercises in this chapter cover finding out what you're good at and want to be doing, while *Focus* (4.8) distils them into a handful of activities. However, there is something else – the underlying principles driving these activities. Your focal activities are about WHAT, your principles say WHY. Be honest. Perhaps it's for power, or to spend more time with your children. Perhaps you want fame or an easy life. Perhaps it's love of God or belief in humanity. Principles don't have to be deep. You might have, 'Have fun every day' or, 'Don't worry about things you can't influence'. Clichés? Maybe, but clichés and fallacies are different: clichés are often true. Most people have three to six major principles driving their activities. Spend a few minutes pulling together what drives you. Stick them at the front of your notebook or on the wall.

Feedback Putting your principles on view has most impact, but they embarrass many people. It's an indictment of our society that we don't like to admit to such things. Hide them away, but understand what you are doing, and why.

Outcome Your principles provide a fixed reference. When reviewing your focal activities, when deciding your priorities, you don't need to read your principles every time, but they are there as a yardstick. It's a great way to keep your time management meaningful.

Variations Although most principles are personal, a couple apply to most people. See *A little chat* (4.28) and *Pareto* (4.26).

Managing yourself	✪✪✪✪
Managing other people	✪✪
Managing externals	✪✪
Business impact	✪✪✪✪
Social impact	✪✪✪✪
Fun	✪✪✪

4.57 | *Filter tips*

Preparation Check your e-mail software.
Running time Five minutes.
Resources E-mail software.
Timescale Ongoing.

If you aren't already using e-mail, see *Mail strain* (4.68). This exercise gives you an electronic helper. Most e-mail software has filters. If yours doesn't seem to, look in the help file. If you don't get any joy, suggest to your IT people that you get a new e-mail package. Filters are dumb personal assistants. They scan the incoming mail, looking for certain attributes.

A good mail filter should be able to:

- Spot a message from a particular individual, flagging it for your attention. This could involve colouring it differently, or showing a special alert. Avoid the latter, you don't want to be distracted.
- Recognize junk and low priority mail and put it in a special folder. Filters aren't safe enough to delete mail. However, you can use known senders (or the traits of junk mail) to put it to one side for a cursory glance. You may also get regular, low priority mail like press releases or newsletters. Divert these to a 'read when I've time' folder, so they don't get in the way.

Feedback Mail filters are only effective if you react appropriately. When you read mail, scan the inbox for highlighted mail first. If you have several mail sessions a day (see *The e-mail of the species* (4.9) for recommendations), only check the low priority folder on the last or first session of the day – resist the temptation to peek.

Outcome Mail filters prevents e-mail taking over, but they can be misused. Play a different tune for each of your friends when they send you a mail and it's more of a hindrance than a help. But stick to these two key operations and the filter will keep your mail manageable.

Variations There are many alternative filtering approaches – it doesn't matter which you use as long as it's non-obtrusive. Don't move priority mail to a separate folder, as this effectively lowers its priority.

Managing yourself	●●
Managing other people	●●●
Managing externals	●●●
Business impact	●●●
Social impact	●●●
Fun	●●

4.58 | *Against the buffers*

Preparation None.
Running time Two minutes.
Resources Diary.
Timescale Weekly.

This associated activity works alongside *Meet yourself half way* (4.17) and the other schedule-oriented techniques. All the others are about making sure you've time in your diary for various activities. This is about making sure you've time for nothing. In a perfect world, you could schedule each meeting, each activity with its follow on travel time so that each runs into the other (actually, it wouldn't be perfect, it would be hell, but you know what I mean). In reality, things overrun or are underestimated and we need buffers. Gaps to allow for variation.

Just spend a minute thinking back over the last couple of weeks. How often did you find that something didn't run to time? Perhaps you were delayed by a traffic jam, or someone else turned up late, or everything took a bit longer than expected... or one of a million other random interferences with precision. Either you go through the day getting later and later, or you build in some slack – buffers.

For near complete safety you probably need around 50 per cent buffer time in your schedule, but with your enhanced time management you could probably get away with applying *Pareto* (4.26) and only having a 20 per cent buffer. Try allowing 20 per cent unplanned time, but be prepared to increase the margin if it's proving effective.

Feedback　Unused buffers aren't a waste of time. You can use them to catch up on lower priority activities that wouldn't otherwise get done.

Outcome　Excessive use of buffers can ruin your scheduling, but by keeping a more realistic allocation your time management can be made more effective.

Variations　You can make buffers vary considerably in length depending on the nature of the activity. Meetings with certain individuals will always overrun. Some journeys are particularly bad when it comes to delays. Use common sense in allocating buffers, rather than a fixed percentage.

Managing yourself	✪✪✪✪
Managing other people	✪✪✪
Managing externals	✪✪
Business impact	✪✪✪✪
Social impact	✪✪✪✪
Fun	✪

4.59 | *Task list stragglers*

Preparation None.
Running time Two minutes.
Resources Diary.
Timescale Weekly.

We all have tasks which don't get completed when we first planned them. It's inevitable. So they get carried forward to the next day or week. But some tasks seem to live in a permanent limbo, never quite making it into the light. When you create a new schedule and task list for the next week, take the opportunity to do something about these stragglers. There are two alternatives – make a task high priority and get it done right away, or drop it from the list. If you choose the first, make sure it is genuinely high priority – if it isn't under way after a day or two, revert to dropping it.

In fact there's a third option, which can be used with a task which is low priority and unpleasant, but has a time dependence that will eventually make it high priority. Often we schedule something like filling in our tax return too early and it becomes one of these stragglers. In this case, it is probably better to schedule it nearer its last possible date and drop it from the task list until then.

Feedback It can be quite difficult to drop an item – after all, you put it in, so it must be worth doing. Just remember the 80:20 rule, see *Pareto* (4.26). You can't do everything. In fact, there are an infinite number of tasks you aren't going to do. What's wrong with having one more? Obviously it depends on why you keep dropping it, but a surprising number can be dropped without consequence.

Outcome Task lists can be killed by stragglers. If your list is full of familiar items that never seem to shift, it is easy to let your eyes skip over it without really taking in what is essential. Pruning the stragglers is an essential to keep it alive.

Variations No real variants.

Managing yourself	✪✪✪✪
Managing other people	✪✪✪
Managing externals	✪✪✪
Business impact	✪✪✪✪
Social impact	✪✪✪✪
Fun	✪

4.60 | *Meeting birth control*

Preparation None.
Running time Five minutes.
Resources Meetings.
Timescale Ongoing.

Other exercises, *Agenda bender* (4.24), *Crowd control* (4.42), *Garbage in, garbage out* (4.27), look at the content of meetings – this is about stopping them breeding. Remember Parkinson's law, 'Work expands to fill the time available for its completion'. Similarly, meetings breed to fill the space in your diary. One control is blocking out time – see *Meet yourself half way* (4.17) – but it is also wise to take direct action. Set yourself a limit on meetings per week, tailoring the number to fit your work pattern. Write it as large as possible in your diary. If you are asked to attend any more meetings, apologize that you are booked up – how about the following week?

With the number of meetings under control, the other requirement is to keep them short. Good agenda management – *Agenda bender* (4.24) – helps, but senior managers can contribute by setting an upper limit (perhaps 90 minutes) after which it is acceptable to walk out if the meeting isn't finished.

Feedback If the time limit gives you a problem, consider this. Performance will be dropping off significantly after 90 minutes. At the very least you need a stretch break. It would also be helpful to use a warm-up or time-out exercise to increase energy in the group (see the companion volume, *Instant Teamwork*). Given such a break, it is reasonable to consider the next session to be a separate meeting. This isn't semantics, it enables each segment to focus on something practical, and brings more clarity to an otherwise over-long session.

Outcome Meetings are valuable, but they need such control to avoid a population explosion.

Variations You could limit yourself to a number of meetings per day, but this isn't as flexible. If you are only in the office once a week it may well be a day full of meetings, but that should be countered by your productivity on other days.

Managing yourself	⊙⊙
Managing other people	⊙⊙⊙⊙
Managing externals	⊙⊙
Business impact	⊙⊙⊙⊙
Social impact	⊙⊙⊙
Fun	⊙

4.61 | *Fluffy phones*

Preparation None.
Running time Two minutes.
Resources Telephone; notebook.
Timescale Ongoing.

Phone calls can eat up large amounts of time. In *Calling by numbers* (4.14), you are encouraged to chunk up your outgoing calls. Here, we look at the content. If you make a call, identify what you want to get out of it. Note the key points and keep them in front of you. You won't work through the points in order – to do so would make the call very stilted – but it will be a guide to what is left to do.

You can use your key points as a checklist or develop branching notes from each point. Most usefully, you can ensure that everything is covered, and be aware when you drift from the point. Social convention requires some deviation. One of the valuable aspects of phone calls is reinforcing your network of contacts, and you cannot afford to be brusque. However, you should be aware of deviation, and bring the conversation back when practical. On the phone you lack many non-verbal cues. Giving short, one-word answers may shut down a topic; otherwise you will have to actively move the subject back into line.

Feedback It may seem artificial, but this approach doesn't interfere with the flow of conversation.

Outcome Applied properly, this technique cuts down on time spent chatting or going over old ground, using your time more effectively.

Variations For incoming calls you have less opportunity to prepare. If your caller doesn't state his or her intentions, ask – as long as it's done politely it won't cause offence and it will enable you to keep the conversation on track. In principle this technique can be used in a social context, and it is useful to make sure important subjects are covered, but bear in mind that the peripheral content is often the main point of a social call and needs to be given a higher priority.

Managing yourself	✪✪✪✪
Managing other people	✪✪✪✪
Managing externals	✪✪
Business impact	✪✪✪✪
Social impact	✪✪
Fun	✪✪

4.62 | *Jump start*

Preparation None.
Running time Five minutes.
Resources None.
Timescale One-off.

For this exercise we are going to spend a couple of minutes thinking about the preparation for your productive day. Jot down the characteristics of an average start. How much sleep do you get? Is it undisturbed? How do you wake up? What happens before you leave the house? What happens on the way to work?

Often these preparatory hours are a mess. We don't get enough sleep. We rush around, shouting at the children or tripping over the cat. We eat a slice of toast as we go out, then spend an hour hitting the steering wheel and shouting at the idiot in front. This isn't great preparation for the day ahead. If you can introduce more calm and better sleep, if you can turn the start of your day into a pleasure rather than a nightmare, you will set yourself up for a more effective day.

Spend the remaining minutes deciding on a few quick actions to make things different. Don't expect overnight change; try feeding them in gradually. They might include making sure you get to bed early enough, getting a reasonable breakfast (at home or out) and making the journey to work less stressful.

Feedback It's easy to think that there's nothing to be done about this area of life. Maybe there isn't a pleasant way of getting to work (unless you get there before 8.00 am or after 10.00 am – is that totally impossible?), but there will always be some aspect that you can improve.

Outcome Starting a task with a positive attitude helps get it completed more effectively.

Variations You can use the positive approach in the evening, too. On the way home, think about positive aspects of the evening. That way, when you get back, you don't arrive gloomy about the day you've had (making for a miserable evening), but looking forward to the pleasant time that you will have.

Managing yourself	✪✪✪✪
Managing other people	✪✪
Managing externals	✪✪
Business impact	✪✪✪✪
Social impact	✪✪✪✪
Fun	✪✪✪

4.63 | *Doggie chocs*

Preparation None.
Running time Two minutes.
Resources None.
Timescale Ongoing.

Some tasks are necessary but difficult to start. Some are *Task list stragglers* (4.59) which are always being bumped down the chain. Others are essential drudgery, or a sort of negative *Cherry picking* (4.32). Faced with such tasks, it helps to employ a touch of psychology. Just as animals are encouraged with a titbit to do things they have no natural urge to do, you can give yourself the promise of a small reward if you get a task done.

It might be the opportunity to do a fun, low priority activity, see *Little treats* (4.36). It might be going out that evening, or literally a titbit – a cake with your coffee or a chocolate bar. Whatever the reward, make sure you use the same techniques as an animal trainer (or parent). The reward must be immediate, beginning as soon as possible after the task is completed. And size doesn't matter; a chocolate bar is as effective for these purposes as an expensive watch.

Feedback This technique sounds ridiculous, because you know what you are doing, so surely it won't work. Not at all. The impact isn't reduced by the knowledge of your actions; the promise of an immediate reward will help you to get something done.

Outcome This technique is great for attacking the ragged edges of your time management. It helps to trim away those tasks that you just can't bring yourself to get on with.

Variations To be effective, the reward has to come soon. This means that a big task needs to be split up into daily deliverables so that you can achieve something every day. You may like to have a slightly larger reward for the overall completion, but shouldn't replace the milestone rewards. You can help other people by giving them similar rewards – if your boss gives you one, you won't have to do it yourself.

Managing yourself	✪✪✪✪
Managing other people	✪
Managing externals	✪
Business impact	✪✪✪✪
Social impact	✪✪✪✪
Fun	✪✪✪✪

4.64 | ***Waiting room***

Preparation None.
Running time Five minutes.
Resources Bag or briefcase.
Timescale Ongoing.

Most of us spend too long waiting for others. You turn up three minutes early and sit in your boss's outer office for 20 minutes before the previous meeting finishes. So you read a business magazine or chat. This same scenario is played out in many other locations. Whether you are sitting in reception or waiting for a seminar to start, time is slipping away.

Some time management experts suggest that you leave a message to say you will be in your office getting some work done, and could they call you when the meeting is about to start. Unfortunately, this is impractical off-site and dangerous on-site. Either you end up playing call-me tag, waiting for everyone to finish a task, or you seriously irritate your boss. Instead, carry a package of portable tasks. Things you can get on with while you wait. It could be your mail, or writing a memo – anything you can do using only the contents of your bag. Make sure you have your task list with you, so you can choose something appropriate.

Feedback You may be regarded as a little strange if others are waiting in the same place. If they don't have tasks to get on with, they might expect you to contribute to their chat. There isn't a right or wrong answer – it depends on who they are and the relevance of the conversation.

Outcome Making use of such unplanned snippets of time is a great way of chipping away at background activities. You are, in effect, generating time from nowhere.

Variations A laptop or palmtop computer makes an ideal mobile task kit. If you are waiting for someone else to arrive, undertake a task that can be stopped at a moment's notice. It doesn't get the meeting off to a good start if your visitor has to watch you finish something off for 10 minutes.

Managing yourself	✪✪✪
Managing other people	✪✪✪✪
Managing externals	✪✪✪
Business impact	✪✪✪✪
Social impact	✪✪✪
Fun	✪✪✪

4.65 | *Train tracks*

Preparation None.
Running time Five minutes.
Resources Bag or briefcase.
Timescale Ongoing.

Travel is a great time waster. This exercise provides one approach to reducing its impact. If you rarely use a train for medium length journeys, think again. You might take the train into a city to avoid traffic congestion or to be environmentally friendly, but there's another reason – it's good time management. Of all the modes of transport, the train is the best suited to thinking and working on the move. There is space, a table, relative peace and a smooth enough motion to read without nausea.

Part one of this technique is using the train more often. Part two is maximizing the value of that time. Don't spend the journey on your mobile, use the train as quiet time. Be unavailable and get some productive work done. It helps if the railway company provides mobile phone free accommodation, so you can avoid other people's calls. Finally, give serious consideration to travelling first class (or equivalent). I even pay my own money to do this. You are less likely to have a small child seated nearby (I've nothing against children, but they aren't conducive to concentration), and you will generally get a seat, even at rush hour. The value of that undisturbed time compared with standing in a corridor is well worth the price.

Feedback   There are always counter arguments to train travel. The time taken to get to the station, the times of the trains, the routes available. Yet most of us could make more use of the train for those mid-length journeys.

Outcome   Travelling by train produces an extra hour or two of productive time and gets you to your destination less stressed.

Variations   If you have to drive, could you share a car with a colleague and have a meeting as you go? Have you a pocket recorder, so you can capture ideas while driving (without crashing into the car in front)?

Managing yourself	❍❍
Managing other people	❍❍
Managing externals	❍❍❍❍
Business impact	❍❍❍❍
Social impact	❍❍
Fun	❍❍

4.66 | *Whosat?*

Preparation Get caller ID installed; purchase appropriate technology.
Running time Two minutes.
Resources Telephone.
Timescale Ongoing.

Incoming telephone calls can be a nightmare. They shatter your concentration and flow, yet they are an essential part of work. Leaving voice mail on isn't a good solution. Many people won't leave a message. Others will be put off. And you will get a reputation for never being there. Incoming calls are also a problem socially. Once you've picked up the phone, good manners require a conversation, even if you are in the middle of a meal, watching a favourite program, doing your Tai-Chi exercises or zapping the enemy in your favourite game.

A handy technical helper is Caller ID (also called Caller Display). This enables you to see the number of an incoming call before picking up the phone. With appropriate technology, you can see the name of the caller or have a computer screen pop up details. Now your options are wider. If the call is unimportant, you can switch to your voice mail. If it is a key customer, you can interrupt your work based on information, rather than an anonymous ring.

Feedback This technology isn't infallible. It could be an unexpected caller on a familiar number. The company ringing you could have an old PABX that doesn't give out extension numbers (still very common). The dialler could withhold their number. But increasingly the information is reliable. A good rule of thumb is to ignore calls with withheld numbers (as opposed to unavailable), as these tend to be salespeople.

Outcome Caller ID filters time-wasting calls. What's more, you can be better prepared for the call. You can also give people a surprise by picking up the phone and saying hello by name.

Variations Some telephone companies charge for caller ID, but it's worth it. Digital mobile phones also have caller ID, so this approach can be used on the move. If a call is diverted from your main phone, the caller ID information passes with it.

Managing yourself	✪✪
Managing other people	✪✪✪✪
Managing externals	✪✪✪✪
Business impact	✪✪✪✪
Social impact	✪✪✪
Fun	✪✪✪

4.67 | *Drawn and quartered*

Preparation None.
Running time Five minutes.
Resources Paper.
Timescale Weekly.

This is an alternative to *Priorities* (4.16) for choosing between tasks. Each is valid – see which works best for you. Split a sheet of paper into four quarters. Label the top left 'Urgent, unimportant', the top right 'Urgent, important', the bottom left 'Not urgent, unimportant' and the bottom right 'Not urgent, important'. Assign each task to a box.

Tasks in the top right box are top priority; you must ensure that their time is protected. Tasks in the top left are time critical, but less important. They often get more time than they should, so get them out of the way as quickly as possible with a tight cut-off. Tasks in the bottom right gradually migrate to the top right as time becomes shorter. The ideal is to catch them early enough to avoid a crisis, but late enough to free up time for other activities. Finally, the bottom left is the area you want to give least time to. Don't let the fact that some of these tasks are enjoyable or easy to do overcome the fact that they are low priority. Give them minimum time.

Feedback A problem with a grid like this is that it is not a fixed object. With time, some (but not all) tasks float upwards. Importance can be time-dependent. Because of this you need to be prepared to redraw regularly – if you can put the diagram in a PC drawing package where you can move the items around the grid flexibly, it will probably prove a better long-term tool.

Outcome Achieving a good balance of priorities lies at the centre of time management. Don't shirk this activity.

Variations This approach can be used as four boxes or as a graph, plotting importance on the horizontal axis and urgency on the vertical axis, so that the further to the right a point appears, the more important it is, and so on.

Managing yourself	✪✪✪✪
Managing other people	✪✪
Managing externals	✪✪✪✪
Business impact	✪✪✪✪
Social impact	✪✪
Fun	✪

4.68 | *Mail strain*

Preparation None.
Running time Two minutes.
Resources E-mail.
Timescale Ongoing.

In another exercise – *Offloading ideas* (4.18) – we look at using electronic mail to prevent an idea hogging valuable processing resources in your brain. This exercise explores other ways to use e-mail. E-mail is very effective for short communications, distributing documents (and other computer files) and asking other people for help or information – using them as a remote resource. For the first part of this exercise, think through your normal activities. What do you do that falls within the scope of e-mail? How do you undertake the activity?

Of the items that don't use e-mail, which could? E-mail won't replace everything, but it can make things a lot quicker. A common activity is printing off a document, taking it to the fax machine, entering a fax number and waiting for transmission (in theory you can leave it, but do you really trust it?). With appropriate e-mail connections, this entire process could be replaced by about five seconds of activity.

Feedback   The power of e-mail is limited by availability at both ends of the interaction. Increasingly this is not a problem, but you do need to make sure that your company allows you to e-mail outside or a lot of the value is lost. Be aware of the potential need for security when sending sensitive information this way.

Outcome   Using an e-mail instead of a fax, or a floppy disk in the post won't make a huge difference to your time management, but it's an ongoing benefit that contributes every day to reducing wasted time.

Variations   Check with correspondents who you don't currently contact via e-mail to see if they have an address. A surprising number will. If you are having trouble thinking of activities, think how you use other means of transport. What do you fax? What do you send by conventional mail? What do you copy onto a floppy disk and transfer that way?

Managing yourself	✪✪✪
Managing other people	✪✪
Managing externals	✪✪✪✪
Business impact	✪✪✪
Social impact	✪✪
Fun	✪✪

4.69 | *Go casual*

Preparation Meeting organized.
Running time Variable.
Resources None.
Timescale One-off.

Meetings eat up time and often don't produce results. Yet meetings are an essential part of business. A high proportion of important decisions and ideas come out of informal meetings. Not a group sat around a board table in a stuffy office, but casual get-togethers around the coffee machine, or chance meetings in the corridor.

Here's a challenge then. Take a meeting you are due to have in the next couple of weeks and move it to a casual location. It might be a coffee bar or a park – I've had one in a car park, but ideally it should be somewhere you can get comfortable, but not have the formal, stuffy surroundings of a meeting room. It should be a meeting that doesn't require lots of technical support like electronic whiteboards or computers. See how it feels. In most cases you will have a much better, more productive meeting.

Feedback Meetings of this sort tend to be shorter than a traditional meeting (the one I had in a car park only lasted 10 minutes, where the usual ones were 90 minutes). They get through more, yet improve interpersonal relations – all to the good both for your business and personal goals. And they make meetings more enjoyable. Surely, anything that can make meetings more enjoyable is worthwhile.

Outcome This isn't a technique you will use for every meeting, but it is worth bringing out in certain cases. For meetings that tend to get bogged down and overrun, for meetings that need a different sort of input, this approach is ideal.

Variations The possible locations can be very varied. To keep it really short, have the meeting standing up – it sounds bizarre, but it is possible. It might mean taking down actions on a pocket recorder and transcribing them later, but it could be worth it if you have a time-keeping problem.

Managing yourself	❍❍
Managing other people	❍❍❍❍
Managing externals	❍❍
Business impact	❍❍❍
Social impact	❍❍
Fun	❍❍❍

4.70 | *Notes with attitude*

Preparation None.
Running time Five minutes.
Resources Notebook.
Timescale Ongoing.

Some notes are scribbled reminders. That's fine. But when taking notes in a meeting or summarizing a report, you need something more structured. The simplest form is an outline. As you add a note, think of a suitable heading. Divide your paper into chunks (some time management system paper comes like this) and assign one or more chunks to each heading. Outlining works particularly well with a word processor if you need to structure notes after the event, or without time pressure.

Unfortunately, notes *are* usually taken under pressure and you don't know how many headings there will be, or how much text for each heading. The best approach, then, is an organic, non-linear form. There are several ways of doing this. One is mind mapping, devised by Tony Buzan. Start with the main subject in the centre of the paper. Draw radial lines from the centre with the main topics written above them, then branch out from these lines with notes or sub-topics. Keep everything to keywords. Good keywords keep notes short, but bring back everything. Alternatives include dotting the paper with topics and radiating from these, or surrounding each topic with a 'cloud' of notes. You can also list the topics down the edge of the paper and radiate sideways. This fits with our left-to-right writing style, but needs an approximate guess at the space each note will take.

Feedback   Try several different approaches until you hit the one that suits you. Conventional, line-by-line writing is so ingrained that you will be tempted to fall back to linear notes. Don't, unless the subject is fixed format (like a name and address).

Outcome   Good note taking encourages you to remember as much as you need. Organic note taking maximizes the chances of getting it right.

Variations   Organic notes are best taken by hand, but there are a number of software packages to help. See Chapter 5.

Managing yourself	✪✪✪✪
Managing other people	✪
Managing externals	✪
Business impact	✪✪✪✪
Social impact	✪✪✪✪
Fun	✪✪✪

4.71 | *Banning homework*

Preparation *Scrap the briefcase* (4.11).
Running time Five minutes.
Resources None.
Timescale Ongoing.

This exercise follows *Scrap the briefcase* (4.11), unless you don't have a bag for taking things home in. Compartmentalization is essential for good time management. With *Scrap the briefcase*, we opened the war on the drift of time from social to work. Now we're going to draw a line. Taking work home is a real enemy of time management. The aim is to avoid it.

In theory this is trivial, just don't take any work home. Full stop. Stay at work until you've finished. If you need to work at the weekend, go into the office. In fact, it's worth going in occasionally at the weekend for the experience; the office atmosphere is usually very different.

Feedback Taking work home has a negative impact on your family and social life and reduces the quality of your work. Don't do it.

Outcome This is vital to overcome. When you take work home, work is in control of your time. Unfortunately it's like stopping smoking. It may take a number of tries.

Variations Taking work home is different from home working, see *Home, sweet home* (4.48). Home workers 'go to the office', it just happens to be a 20 second commute away. There's nothing wrong with working on the train, but make sure that the tasks are easy to switch off so you aren't tempted to continue at home. Sometimes you have to work in the evening. Perhaps you want to get home and see the children, then do some work. Surely you can take work home then? If possible, no. Return to the workplace. If commuting times make this impractical, have a specific work environment in the home. Don't go in there as soon as you get home. Have your social time, then make it clear you are 'going to work'. If you must work in the evening and can't get in to the office, convert to home working.

Managing yourself	●●●●
Managing other people	●●●
Managing externals	●●●●
Business impact	●●
Social impact	●●●●
Fun	●●●

4.72 | *Caught in the web*

Preparation None.
Running time Five minutes.
Resources Internet connection.
Timescale One-off.

It's not just the computer on your desk – see *PC plod* (4.53) – that can hog time, so can the Internet. A lot has been written about the dangers of the World Wide Web. Much of this concerns pornography or time wasted exploring. In fact, the problems of time wasting are exaggerated. After all, just become someone isn't surfing the net doesn't mean they would otherwise be fully productive. And no value is given to the information culled this way. However, you won't want to waste your own time on the Web.

Put together an Internet strategy. Have a cut-off time, perhaps half an hour, after which you will come off-line and give some thought to what you have retrieved. This may need to be reinforced with a kitchen timer. Next, have a single, clear objective. If something else comes up, make a note of it, but don't be distracted. Finally, make use of tools that allow you to revisit the pages you have seen off-line, and of tools to search and summarize sites. This way you can condense the search effort and come back to your results at a later date.

Feedback Part of the reasons for the Web's ability to eat time is its eclectic nature. This strategy is aimed at getting a straight answer to a specific requirement – but do allow yourself occasional free-access sessions. It could give you surprising insights.

Outcome The Internet is a powerful tool, but like any powerful tool it can be dangerous if misused. This exercise provides a way of getting value from the Web while reducing the danger.

Variations If you have a number of topics, it is generally better to research each separately, but if you find significant overlaps, go with the flow – just make sure that you can separate the outputs after the event. For more guidance, see *Mining the Internet*, Brian Clegg (Kogan Page, 1999).

Managing yourself	❍❍❍
Managing other people	❍
Managing externals	❍❍❍❍
Business impact	❍❍❍❍
Social impact	❍❍❍❍
Fun	❍❍❍

5

OTHER SOURCES

MORE TIME MANAGEMENT

Instant Time Management is all you need to take control of your time, and the drip-feed approach is more likely to be effective than an immediate life transformation or glossy ring-binder system. However, there are times when it is helpful to take a wider view or use other resources. This chapter details some extra sources of information and help in improving your time management. It does not aim to be comprehensive, but should provide a useful starting point if you would like to expand your time management expertise.

WEB SOURCES

The World Wide Web has become the universal source for assistance and information. You will find web addresses in the references to systems and software below. To find more general information, input 'time management' into a search engine or Web index and browse around. Here are a couple of the best-known addresses to get you started:
http://www.altavista.com
http://www.yahoo.com

BOOKS

Brian Clegg, *The Chameleon Manager*, Butterworth Heinemann, 1998
This book takes the concept of time management into the wider sphere of gaining the skills needed to thrive in the workplace of the new millennium. It identifies management of creativity, communication and knowledge as the key requirements to working your way, and includes a different slant on time management from this perspective.

Jane Smith, *How to be a better... Time Manager*, Kogan Page, 1997
An Industrial Society sponsored volume, Smith's book takes an easy-to-read, no-nonsense approach to time management. A fair number of check lists and little questionnaires to fill in along the way, if you like that style.

Marion E Hayes, *Make Every Minute Count*, Kogan Page, 1996
In the quick-fire *Better Management Skills* series, this is the only one of these books that is US written – but the subject varies little between countries. Even more check-

lists and questionnaires than Smith's book, this is an excellent way of getting started on the subject.

Lothar J Seiwert, *Managing Your Time*, Kogan Page, 1989
A very visual book with lots of diagrams and plans and cartoons – it'll either impress you (as it has apparently more than 300,000 readers) or leave you cold. Particularly helpful if you like very specific guidance and information as juicy snippets.

Ted Johns, *Perfect Time Management*, Arrow, 1994
A handy pocket book giving an overview of time management practice from a very pragmatic viewpoint. Varies between background and quite a lot of detail (eg, suggested forms for the agenda of a meeting).

SYSTEMS

Although systems can be dangerously addictive, taking up more time than they release, some find them effective aids to time management. This section lists some of the better-known systems, without making any recommendations.

DAY-TIMER

Effective planner/diary system that puts all the basic information on a two page spread. **http://www.daytimer.com**

Day-Timers Europe: Freepost ANG6275, Hertford SG13 7YE (0800-542-0520)
Day-Timers, Inc: One Day-Timer Plaza, Lehigh Valley, PA 18195-1551 (800-225-5005)

FILOFAX

The old original in the personal organizer market. Although *Filofax* doesn't have its own time management system, the ring binders and stationery do everything required without any philosophical baggage. **http://www.filofax.com**
Filofax Group PLC: Waverley House 8-12, Noel Street, London W1V 3PB (0171-432-3000)

TIME MANAGER INTERNATIONAL

Probably the most evangelical of the time management system providers, *TMI* shows its Scandinavian roots in a certain earnestness, and has a tendency to produce far too many different stationery types, but its heart is in the right place and the key area/ task break down is well structured. **http://www.tmiworld.com**

TMI UK: 50 High Street, Henley-in-Arden, Solihull, West Midlands B95 5AN, (01564-794100)
TMI US: 181 Carlos Drive, Suite 102, San Rafael, California 94903, (415 499-5500)

TIME/SYSTEM INTERNATIONAL

Another Scandinavian system supplier, again quite heavy on the different forms, but with a slightly less philosophical approach than *TMI*. Breaks down activities into a lot of detail. Slightly larger ring-binder format, handy for those who don't have small writing. **http://www.timesystem.com**

Time/System UK: 6 Vincent Avenue, Crownhill Business Centre, Milton Keynes, MK8 0AB (01908-263333)
Time/System US: 265 Main Street, Agawam, Massachusetts 01001 (800 637-9942

SOFTWARE

Software dates almost as quickly as World Wide Web references, but these products currently represent a good cross-section of the software products available to support your time management. Check the web sites for up-to-date information.

GENERAL PERSONAL INFORMATION MANAGERS

Microsoft Outlook (www.microsoft.com)
Widely available as it is supplied with the *Microsoft Office* suite, *Outlook* is a very effective package for the time manager, combining diary, contact list, task list, journal (time-based list of files used, etc), notes, e-mail and fax. Mostly intuitive and easy to use.

Lotus Organizer (www.lotus.com)
Before *Outlook*, *Organizer* was the number one PIM (personal information manager) and it is still very attractive. Very much based on the look of a traditional personal organizer, but with additional electronic functionality. Diary, task list, address book, calls, planner, and notepad.

OfficeTalk (www.sareen.com)
A different approach from this British product. It provides PIM facilities for groups of five to 500 people, allowing more sophisticated group sharing of information than either of the competitors. Diary, planner, cut-down project manager, task list, address book, contact management and e-mail. Significantly more complex than either of the other products, but more group functionality.

TIME MANAGEMENT SYSTEMS

TaskTimer (www.timesystem.com) – Time/System International
Automates the *Time/System* approach to time management. Probably closest to *OfficeTalk* in functionality, but with a very strong time management structure (activities, tasks, and so on).

Time Manager (www.tmi.co.uk) – Time Manager
Automates the *Time Manager* approach, particularly for hand-held electronic organizers.

ORGANIC NOTE TAKING

VisiMap (www.coco.co.uk)
VisiMap is a PC package to help with note taking. It produces a mind map that is very easy to add to and edit. Although less visual than a hand-drawn map, it is very quick to put a map together and automatically balances the layout of the map. Exports to *Word* and other packages.

MindMan (www.mindman.com)
Another mind mapping package, *MindMan* has a better graphical approach than *VisiMap*, so it produces more visual maps, better for taking notes from a book (say) when learning information. However, it isn't quite as easy to pour information into, so isn't as good for live note-taking from a discussion or brain dumping.

Creativity Unleashed Limited (www.cul.co.uk)
Software changes with time. The Creativity Unleashed Limited web site has up-to-date links to other sites on visual mapping and other techniques appropriate for time management.

APPENDIX 1:
THE FRAMEWORK

WHAT FRAMEWORK?

The *Instant* series of books is designed to work the way you want to work – it's up to you. You might prefer to dip in as and when you like. If so, that's fine. Appendix 2 has some tables that can help. Alternatively you may prefer some form of structure. This appendix contains a couple of frameworks.

The first section structures the exercises by their timescale. Exercises which are best done daily, weekly, monthly and annually are grouped together to tick off when you've got them set up in your diary. So they don't slip through the cracks, there is also a list of the one-off and ongoing exercises.

The second section structures all 72 exercises into five-part packages. As each exercise is very short, everyone should be able to fit one in each working day, giving you a weekly course to time management perfection. Alternatively, you could accelerate all the way up to a package a day. Framework or freestyle – the choice is yours.

DAILY, WEEKLY, MONTHLY AND ANNUALLY – YOUR MAKEOVER PLAN

Note that some of the 'weekly' exercises are a mix between weekly and daily. For instance, you may well set up your task list for the week, but you will be consulting it, changing it and checking things off throughout the week.

Ref.	Title	Completed	Ref.	Title	Completed
Daily			*Monthly*		
4.14	Calling by numbers	☐	4.8	Focus	☐
4.31	Paper mountains	☐	4.30	Letting go	☐
4.46	Going walkabout	☐	4.39	We have contact	☐
Weekly			*Annually*		
4.10	The top 10 list	☐	4.1	Talent spotting	☐
4.13	Chunking	☐	4.2	If I were a rich man	☐
4.16	Priorities	☐	4.4	Obstacle map	☐
4.17	Meet yourself half way	☐	4.21	A personal project	☐
4.25	Tasks, tasks	☐	4.29	Penalizing pen pushing	☐
4.37	Scheduling admin	☐	4.34	Failure rate	☐
4.58	Against the buffers	☐			
4.59	Task list stragglers	☐			
4.67	Drawn and quartered	☐			

One-off/ongoing

Ref.	Title		Ref.	Title	
4.3	Dream day	☐	4.43	Rampant reading	☐
4.5	What's it worth?	☐	4.44	We don't deliver	☐
4.6	Where'd it go?	☐	4.45	The secretary's secret	☐
4.7	Hot spots	☐	4.47	Deflecting distraction	☐
4.9	The e-mail of the species	☐	4.48	Home, sweet home	☐
4.11	Scrap the briefcase	☐	4.49	Be prepared	☐
4.12	Why not no?	☐	4.50	Nota bene	☐
4.15	Quiet corners	☐	4.51	Delegation difficulties	☐
4.18	Offloading ideas	☐	4.52	Reading up	☐
4.19	No, I can	☐	4.53	PC plod	☐
4.20	No action, no report	☐	4.54	It's mine	☐
4.22	Travel times	☐	4.55	TV turn-off	☐
4.23	Telephone tag	☐	4.56	Principles	☐
4.24	Agenda bender	☐	4.57	Filter tips	☐
4.26	Pareto	☐	4.60	Meeting birth control	☐
4.27	Garbage in, garbage out	☐	4.61	Fluffy phones	☐
4.28	A little chat	☐	4.62	Jump start	☐
4.32	Cherry picking	☐	4.63	Doggie chocs	☐
4.33	How wide is your door?	☐	4.64	Waiting room	☐
4.35	A file in a cake	☐	4.65	Train tracks	☐
4.36	Little treats	☐	4.66	Whosat?	☐
4.38	The red hat	☐	4.68	Mail strain	☐
4.40	Floor plan	☐	4.69	Go casual	☐
4.41	How long?	☐	4.70	Notes with attitude	☐
4.42	Crowd control	☐	4.71	Banning homework	☐
			4.72	Caught in the web	☐

THE WHOLE WORKS

In the table below, the exercises are divided into packages of five. This makes it easy to work through the book as a one-a-day course, each package taking a week. Alternatively, you might speed things up by getting more packages in – it's up to you.

Ref.	Title	Completed	Ref.	Title	Completed
Package 1			*Package 2*		
4.1	Talent spotting	☐	4.6	Where'd it go?	☐
4.2	If I were a rich man	☐	4.7	Hot spots	☐
4.3	Dream day	☐	4.8	Focus	☐
4.4	Obstacle map	☐	4.9	The e-mail of the species	☐
4.5	What's it worth?	☐	4.10	The top 10 list	☐

Package 3
4.11   Scrap the briefcase   ☐
4.12   Why not no?   ☐
4.13   Chunking   ☐
4.14   Calling by numbers   ☐
4.15   Quiet corners   ☐

Package 4
4.16   Priorities   ☐
4.17   Meet yourself half way   ☐
4.18   Offloading ideas   ☐
4.19   No, I can   ☐
4.20   No action, no report   ☐

Package 5
4.21   A personal project   ☐
4.22   Travel times   ☐
4.23   Telephone tag   ☐
4.24   Agenda bender   ☐
4.25   Tasks, tasks   ☐

Package 6
4.26   Pareto   ☐
4.27   Garbage in, garbage out   ☐
4.28   A little chat   ☐
4.29   Penalizing pen pushing   ☐
4.30   Letting go   ☐

Package 7
4.31   Paper mountains   ☐
4.32   Cherry picking   ☐
4.33   How wide is your door?   ☐
4.34   Failure rate   ☐
4.35   A file in a cake   ☐

Package 8
4.36   Little treats   ☐
4.37   Scheduling admin   ☐
4.38   The red hat   ☐
4.39   We have contact   ☐
4.40   Floor plan   ☐

Package 9
4.41   How long?   ☐
4.42   Crowd control   ☐
4.43   Rampant reading   ☐

4.44   We don't deliver   ☐
4.45   The secretary's secret   ☐

Package 10
4.46   Going walkabout   ☐
4.47   Deflecting distraction   ☐
4.48   Home, sweet home   ☐
4.49   Be prepared   ☐
4.50   Nota bene   ☐

Package 11
4.51   Delegation difficulties   ☐
4.52   Reading up   ☐
4.53   PC plod   ☐
4.54   It's mine   ☐
4.55   TV turn-off   ☐

Package 12
4.56   Principles   ☐
4.57   Filter tips   ☐
4.58   Against the buffers   ☐
4.59   Task list stragglers   ☐
4.60   Meeting birth control   ☐

Package 13
4.61   Fluffy phones   ☐
4.62   Jump start   ☐
4.63   Doggie chocs   ☐
4.64   Waiting room   ☐
4.65   Train tracks   ☐

Package 14
4.66   Whosat?   ☐
4.67   Drawn and quartered   ☐
4.68   Mail strain   ☐
4.69   Go casual   ☐
4.70   Notes with attitude   ☐

Package 15
4.71   Banning homework   ☐
4.72   Caught in the web   ☐
+ check your daily, weekly,
monthly and annual actions

APPENDIX 2: THE SELECTOR

SELECTION TABLES

This appendix contains a series of tables to help to select an exercise to do right now. The first table, the random selector is for when you'd like something unexpected. The other tables help highlight a particular characteristic of an exercise, like applicability to business, or fun.

THE RANDOM SELECTOR

Take a watch with a second hand and note the number the second hand is pointing at now. Take that number technique from the list of 60 below. The first five techniques in Chapter 4 are not included, as they are intended to provide the background for all the rest; consider doing these first before dipping in at random. A few of the exercises assume you have completed another already – if you hit one of these and haven't done the preliminaries, either do the other exercise first or pick again.

No.	Ref.	Title	No.	Ref.	Title
1	4.6	Where'd it go?	23	4.31	Paper mountains
2	4.7	Hot spots	24	4.32	Cherry picking
3	4.8	Focus	25	4.33	How wide is your door?
4	4.9	The e-mail of the species	26	4.34	Failure rate
5	4.10	The top 10 list	27	4.35	A file in a cake
6	4.11	Scrap the briefcase	28	4.36	Little treats
7	4.12	Why not no?	29	4.37	Scheduling admin
8	4.13	Chunking	30	4.38	The red hat
9	4.14	Calling by numbers	31	4.39	We have contact
10	4.15	Quiet corners	32	4.40	Floor plan
11	4.16	Priorities	33	4.41	How long?
12	4.17	Meet yourself half way	34	4.43	Rampant reading
13	4.18	Offloading ideas	35	4.44	We don't deliver
14	4.20	No action, no report	36	4.46	Going walkabout
15	4.21	A personal project	37	4.47	Deflecting distraction
16	4.22	Travel times	38	4.48	Home, sweet home
17	4.23	Telephone tag	39	4.49	Be prepared
18	4.25	Tasks, tasks	40	4.50	Nota bene
19	4.26	Pareto	41	4.51	Delegation difficulties
20	4.28	A little chat	42	4.52	Reading up
21	4.29	Penalizing pen pushing	43	4.53	PC plod
22	4.30	Letting go	44	4.54	It's mine

TECHNIQUES IN TIMING ORDER

This table sorts the techniques by the suggested timings. Those at the top take the longest, those towards the bottom are the quickest.

Ref.	Title	Ref	Title
Variable		4.4	Obstacle map
4.27	Garbage in, garbage out	4.5	What's it worth?
4.69	Go casual	4.6	Where'd it go?
		4.7	Hot spots
15 minutes		4.9	The e-mail of the species
4.35	A file in a cake	4.10	The top 10 list
		4.12	Why not no?
10 minutes		4.13	Chunking
4.8	Focus	4.14	Calling by numbers
4.11	Scrap the briefcase	4.15	Quiet corners
4.19	No, I can	4.16	Priorities
4.21	A personal project	4.20	No action, no report
4.29	Penalizing pen pushing	4.22	Travel times
4.30	Letting go	4.23	Telephone tag
4.34	Failure rate	4.25	Tasks, tasks
4.39	We have contact	4.26	Pareto
4.43	Rampant reading	4.28	A little chat
4.45	The secretary's secret	4.31	Paper mountains
4.46	Going walkabout	4.32	Cherry picking
4.48	Home, sweet home	4.33	How wide is your door?
4.49	Be prepared	4.36	Little treats
		4.37	Scheduling admin
Five minutes		4.40	Floor plan
4.1	Talent spotting	4.41	How long?
4.2	If I were a rich man	4.44	We don't deliver
4.3	Dream day	4.51	Delegation difficulties

4.52	Reading up		*Two minutes*	
4.53	PC plod		4.17	Meet yourself half way
4.54	It's mine		4.18	Offloading ideas
4.56	Principles		4.24	Agenda bender
4.57	Filter tips		4.38	The red hat
4.60	Meeting birth control		4.42	Crowd control
4.62	Jump start		4.47	Deflecting distraction
4.64	Waiting room		4.50	Nota bene
4.65	Train tracks		4.55	TV turn-off
4.67	Drawn and quartered		4.58	Against the buffers
4.70	Notes with attitude		4.59	Task list stragglers
4.71	Banning homework		4.61	Fluffy phones
4.72	Caught in the web		4.63	Doggie chocs
			4.66	Whosat?
			4.68	Mail strain

TECHNIQUES IN MANAGING YOURSELF ORDER

This table sorts the techniques by the *Managing yourself* star rating. Those at the top have most stars, those at the bottom least.

Ref.	Title		Ref.	Title
OOOO			4.28	A little chat
4.1	Talent spotting		4.30	Letting go
4.2	If I were a rich man		4.32	Cherry picking
4.3	Dream day		4.33	How wide is your door?
4.4	Obstacle map		4.34	Failure rate
4.5	What's it worth?		4.35	A file in a cake
4.7	Hot spots		4.36	Little treats
4.8	Focus		4.37	Scheduling admin
4.10	The top 10 list		4.41	How long?
4.12	Why not no?		4.43	Rampant reading
4.13	Chunking		4.44	We don't deliver
4.14	Calling by numbers		4.48	Home, sweet home
4.16	Priorities		4.50	Nota bene
4.17	Meet yourself half way		4.51	Delegation difficulties
4.18	Offloading ideas		4.52	Reading up
4.19	No, I can		4.54	It's mine
4.21	A personal project		4.56	Principles
4.25	Tasks, tasks		4.58	Against the buffers
4.26	Pareto		4.59	Task list stragglers

4.61	Fluffy phones
4.62	Jump start
4.63	Doggie chocs
4.67	Drawn and quartered
4.70	Notes with attitude
4.71	Banning homework

❂❂❂
4.6	Where'd it go?
4.9	The e-mail of the species
4.11	Scrap the briefcase
4.15	Quiet corners
4.20	No action, no report
4.22	Travel times
4.23	Telephone tag
4.27	Garbage in, garbage out
4.29	Penalizing pen pushing
4.39	We have contact
4.40	Floor plan
4.45	The secretary's secret

4.53	PC plod
4.55	TV turn-off
4.64	Waiting room
4.68	Mail strain
4.72	Caught in the web

❂❂
4.24	Agenda bender
4.31	Paper mountains
4.38	The red hat
4.42	Crowd control
4.46	Going walkabout
4.47	Deflecting distraction
4.49	Be prepared
4.57	Filter tips
4.60	Meeting birth control
4.65	Train tracks
4.66	Whosat?
4.69	Go casual

TECHNIQUES IN MANAGING OTHERS ORDER

This table sorts the techniques by the *Managing others* star rating. Those at the top have most stars, those at the bottom least.

Ref.	Title
❂❂❂❂	
4.6	Where'd it go?
4.9	The e-mail of the species
4.10	The top 10 list
4.12	Why not no?
4.15	Quiet corners
4.17	Meet yourself half way
4.19	No, I can
4.20	No action, no report
4.23	Telephone tag
4.24	Agenda bender
4.27	Garbage in, garbage out
4.29	Penalizing pen pushing
4.30	Letting go
4.33	How wide is your door?
4.38	The red hat

Ref.	Title
4.39	We have contact
4.42	Crowd control
4.45	The secretary's secret
4.46	Going walkabout
4.47	Deflecting distraction
4.48	Home, sweet home
4.49	Be prepared
4.51	Delegation difficulties
4.60	Meeting birth control
4.61	Fluffy phones
4.64	Waiting room
4.66	Whosat?
4.69	Go casual
❂❂❂	
4.14	Calling by numbers
4.26	Pareto

Ref.	Title	Ref.	Title
4.28	A little chat	4.52	Reading up
4.31	Paper mountains	4.56	Principles
4.34	Failure rate	4.62	Jump start
4.54	It's mine	4.65	Train tracks
4.57	Filter tips	4.67	Drawn and quartered
4.58	Against the buffers	4.68	Mail strain
4.59	Task list stragglers	✪	
4.71	Banning homework	4.1	Talent spotting
✪✪		4.3	Dream day
4.2	If I were a rich man	4.7	Hot spots
4.4	Obstacle map	4.11	Scrap the briefcase
4.5	What's it worth?	4.18	Offloading ideas
4.8	Focus	4.21	A personal project
4.13	Chunking	4.22	Travel times
4.16	Priorities	4.32	Cherry picking
4.25	Tasks, tasks	4.36	Little treats
4.35	A file in a cake	4.50	Nota bene
4.37	Scheduling admin	4.53	PC plod
4.40	Floor plan	4.55	TV turn-off
4.41	How long?	4.63	Doggie chocs
4.43	Rampant reading	4.70	Notes with attitude
4.44	We don't deliver	4.72	Caught in the web

TECHNIQUES IN MANAGING EXTERNALS ORDER

This table sorts the techniques by the *Managing externals* star rating. Those at the top have most stars, those at the bottom least.

Ref.	Title	Ref.	Title
✪✪✪✪		4.65	Train tracks
4.9	The e-mail of the species	4.66	Whosat?
4.11	Scrap the briefcase	4.67	Drawn and quartered
4.15	Quiet corners	4.68	Mail strain
4.22	Travel times	4.71	Banning homework
4.29	Penalizing pen pushing	4.72	Caught in the web
4.31	Paper mountains	✪✪✪	
4.35	A file in a cake	4.6	Where'd it go?
4.37	Scheduling admin	4.14	Calling by numbers
4.40	Floor plan	4.26	Pareto
4.48	Home, sweet home	4.30	Letting go
4.53	PC plod	4.33	How wide is your door?
4.55	TV turn-off	4.34	Failure rate

4.43	Rampant reading	4.47	Deflecting distraction
4.45	The secretary's secret	4.50	Nota bene
4.46	Going walkabout	4.51	Delegation difficulties
4.49	Be prepared	4.54	It's mine
4.52	Reading up	4.56	Principles
4.57	Filter tips	4.58	Against the buffers
4.59	Task list stragglers	4.60	Meeting birth control
4.64	Waiting room	4.61	Fluffy phones
✪✪		4.62	Jump start
4.2	If I were a rich man	4.69	Go casual
4.4	Obstacle map	✪	
4.5	What's it worth?	4.1	Talent spotting
4.8	Focus	4.3	Dream day
4.13	Chunking	4.7	Hot spots
4.16	Priorities	4.10	The top 10 list
4.17	Meet yourself half way	4.12	Why not no?
4.20	No action, no report	4.18	Offloading ideas
4.21	A personal project	4.19	No, I can
4.23	Telephone tag	4.24	Agenda bender
4.25	Tasks, tasks	4.28	A little chat
4.27	Garbage in, garbage out	4.36	Little treats
4.32	Cherry picking	4.38	The red hat
4.39	We have contact	4.42	Crowd control
4.41	How long?	4.63	Doggie chocs
4.44	We don't deliver	4.70	Notes with attitude

TECHNIQUES IN BUSINESS IMPACT ORDER

This table sorts the techniques by the *Business impact* star rating. Those at the top have most stars, those at the bottom least.

Ref.	Title	Ref.	Title
✪✪✪✪		4.10	The top 10 list
4.1	Talent spotting	4.12	Why not no?
4.2	If I were a rich man	4.13	Chunking
4.3	Dream day	4.14	Calling by numbers
4.4	Obstacle map	4.15	Quiet corners
4.5	What's it worth?	4.16	Priorities
4.6	Where'd it go?	4.17	Meet yourself half way
4.8	Focus	4.18	Offloading ideas
4.9	The e-mail of the species	4.19	No, I can

4.20	No action, no report	4.52	Reading up
4.23	Telephone tag	4.53	PC plod
4.24	Agenda bender	4.56	Principles
4.25	Tasks, tasks	4.58	Against the buffers
4.26	Pareto	4.59	Task list stragglers
4.27	Garbage in, garbage out	4.60	Meeting birth control
4.29	Penalizing pen pushing	4.61	Fluffy phones
4.30	Letting go	4.62	Jump start
4.31	Paper mountains	4.63	Doggie chocs
4.32	Cherry picking	4.64	Waiting room
4.33	How wide is your door?	4.65	Train tracks
4.34	Failure rate	4.66	Whosat?
4.35	A file in a cake	4.67	Drawn and quartered
4.36	Little treats	4.70	Notes with attitude
4.37	Scheduling admin	4.72	Caught in the web
4.38	The red hat	✪✪✪	
4.39	We have contact	4.28	A little chat
4.40	Floor plan	4.7	Hot spots
4.41	How long?	4.11	Scrap the briefcase
4.42	Crowd control	4.22	Travel times
4.43	Rampant reading	4.54	It's mine
4.44	We don't deliver	4.57	Filter tips
4.45	The secretary's secret	4.68	Mail strain
4.46	Going walkabout	4.69	Go casual
4.47	Deflecting distraction	✪✪	
4.48	Home, sweet home	4.21	A personal project
4.49	Be prepared	4.55	TV turn-off
4.50	Nota bene	4.71	Banning homework
4.51	Delegation difficulties		

TECHNIQUES IN SOCIAL IMPACT ORDER

This table sorts the techniques by the *Social impact* star rating. Those at the top have most stars, those at the bottom least.

Ref.	Title	Ref.	Title
✪✪✪✪		4.8	Focus
4.1	Talent spotting	4.12	Why not no?
4.2	If I were a rich man	4.13	Chunking
4.3	Dream day	4.16	Priorities
4.4	Obstacle map	4.19	No, I can
4.5	What's it worth?	4.21	A personal project

TECHNIQUES IN FUN ORDER

This table sorts the techniques by the *Fun* star rating. Those at the top have most stars, those at the bottom least.

UNIVERSITY OF LINCOLN

Printed in the United Kingdom
by Lightning Source UK Ltd.
121572UK00001B/682-720/A

9 780749 429638